ALTON
BROWN

TOP CHEFS

TOP
CHEFS

ALTON
BROWN

JOHN F. GRABOWSKI

Produced by OTTN Publishing, Stockton, New Jersey

Eldorado Ink
PO Box 100097
Pittsburgh, PA 15233
www.eldoradoink.com

CPSIA compliance information: Batch#TC010112-1. For further
information, contact Eldorado Ink at info@eldoradoink.com.

First printing

1 3 5 7 9 8 6 4 2

Library of Congress Cataloging-in-Publication Data

Grabowski, John F.
  Alton Brown / John F. Grabowski.
      p. cm. — (Top chefs)
  Includes bibliographical references and index.
  ISBN 978-1-61900-007-0 (hc)
  ISBN 978-1-61900-008-7 (pb)
  ISBN 978-1-61900-009-4 (ebook)
  1. Brown, Alton, 1962—-Juvenile literature. 2. Cooks—California—Los
Angeles—Biography—Juvenile literature. 3. Celebrity chefs—
California—Los Angeles—Biography—Juvenile literature. I. Title.
  TX649.B69G73 2012
  641.5092—dc23
  [B]

                                    2011044886

For information about custom editions, special sales, or
premiums, please contact our special sales department at
info@eldoradoink.com.

TABLE OF CONTENTS

Vapor

Popped Corn

$S = Slope$
$F = Friction$
$G = Gravity$

$k =$

P

$$k + r^3 \frac{\sqrt{PZ}}{.73}$$

Alton Brown's Good Eats *program takes a humorous yet educational look at the science behind food and cooking.*

CHAPTER ONE

"GREAT CHEESY FUN"

On April 4, 2007, the University of Georgia in Athens announced the 35 winners of the 2006 Peabody Awards. This prestigious honor is given for outstanding achievement in electronic media, including broadcast television, cable, and radio. "The Award is determined by one criterion—'Excellence,'" proclaims the mission statement on the Peabody website. In 2007 the Peabody panel of academics, television critics, and media-industry professionals honored for the first time a program from the cable television channel Food Network. The judges announced that one of the Peabody Awards would go to *Good Eats*, a quirky cooking show that explored food, science, history, and culture. *Good Eats* was the creation of Alton Brown, who not only wrote and produced each show, but also starred as host of the program.

GOOD EATS

Since it first premiered in July 1999 on the Food Network, *Good Eats* had taught millions of people the science and technique behind cooking. Brown presented the basics in a goofy, fun format, using humor to educate viewers about the "why" of cooking, the history of food, and the use of various kinds of equipment for food preparation, baking, and roasting. To teach his "lessons" Brown relied on elements of pop culture and comedy. He used puppets and props, as well as fictional characters like the "Mother of Culinary Invention" and real-life scientific authorities, such as a nutritional anthropologist and dieticians.

The major focus was to present information in a fun way. In an interview with National Public Radio, Brown explained, "*Good Eats* isn't about food, it's about entertainment. If, however, we can virally infect you with knowledge or interest, then all the better."

WHAT IS A PEABODY?

The winners of the Peabody Awards for 2006 were announced during a ceremony in the Peabody Gallery on the campus of the University of Georgia. Among the programs being honored—in addition to *Good Eats*—were the popular prime-time series *Scrubs*, *Ugly Betty*, *The Office*, and *Friday Night Lights*.

The Peabody Award is named for George Foster Peabody, a successful Georgia-born investment banker and philanthropist who donated a large portion of his fortune to the University of Georgia in Athens. After his death, the National Association of Broadcasters (NAB) formed a committee to establish an award in recognition of excellence in radio broadcasting. One of its members approached John E.

George Foster Peabody (1852–1938) made a fortune as an investment banker during the late 19th and early 20th centuries. In 1906, the year before the top photo was taken, Peabody retired from business to focus on public service and charitable works.

Drewry, dean of the Grady College of Journalism and Mass Communication at the University of Georgia, about sponsoring the award.

The NAB approved the plan in 1940, and the awards were named for Peabody in appreciation of his contributions to the university. Marjorie Peabody Waite, the philanthropist's adopted daughter, commissioned the design of the medal, which featured his name and image. The first awards, for excellence in radio programs broadcast in 1940, were presented in 1941. Awards for television broadcasting were added in 1948, and

The first Peabody Awards ceremony, held in 1941, honored five radio programs. As of 2011 the largest number of awards presented in a single year is 36.

the first cable award was presented in 1981. Web content was honored soon after. The Peabody Awards have since become synonymous with excellence in the field of electronic media.

Over the years Peabody Awards have honored a wide range of personalities as well as programs. People who have received the award include talk show host Oprah Winfrey, television and radio host Larry King, screenwriter and television producer Rod Serling, and broadcast journalist Walter Cronkite. Winning programs have included *The Ed Sullivan Show*, Edward R. Murrow's *See It Now*, *The Daily Show with Jon Stewart*, and *Dora the Explorer*.

THE FRENCH CHEF

The first cooking show to win a Peabody Award was a program hosted by Julia Child (1912–2004). She introduced French cuisine to the American public through her first cookbook, *Mastering the Art of French Cooking*. The popularity of that book led to her television show *The French Chef*, which debuted on Boston's WGBH-TV in 1963. The show was an immediate success, and won a Peabody in 1964.

The French Chef was taped live. Because it was broadcast uncut and unedited, Child had to deal with occasional mistakes on the air. But her passion for food and ability to smooth over accidents ensured her popularity with viewers. She would write many more cookbooks and host several other television series over the years.

The 2009 film *Julie and Julia*, which starred Meryl Streep as Julia Child, told the story of a young New Yorker who attempted in one year to cook all 524 recipes in *Mastering the Art of French Cooking*. The film received mostly positive reviews.

A sign that hung over the *Good Eats* studio door said, "Laughing brains are more absorbent." In other words, people learn better when they are entertained.

The number of winners chosen from the more than 1,000 entries received each year averages from 25 to 35. Entries are considered within one of seven categories: news; entertainment; programs for children; education; documentary; public service; and individuals, institutions, or organizations.

THE 2006 PEABODY AWARDS

Brown's publicist, Athalie White, submitted *Good Eats* as a candidate for the award, but Alton has said that he never dreamed it could win. On its website, the Peabody Awards justified why his program deserved the recognition:

> What sets Brown and his *Good Eats* gang apart is how much they know and include in their half-hour programs about history, anthropology, math, chemistry, physics and popular culture. . . . Whether Brown is advising Okra's agent, Syd, on how to make his slimy client more popular, demonstrating how NOT to deep-fry a turkey, or describing ancient popcorn-popping methods, his show is a feast of puns, goofy props and good advice. For being omnivorously educational and great cheesy fun, *Good Eats* receives a Peabody.

The 66th Annual Peabody Awards took place on June 4, 2007. The awards were presented at a luncheon at the Waldorf Astoria Hotel in New York City. Sportscaster Bob Costas served as master of ceremonies for the event. Because of a previous commitment, Brown was unable to be there. But Dana Popoff, the producer of *Good Eats*, and Marion Laney, the director of photography, attended in his place. They brought with them a video message from Alton in which he expressed his feelings in being honored. "I'm blown away to be receiving a Peabody," he said. "That's not something that I ever thought would happen in my lifetime."

The Peabody was not the first recognition that Alton Brown has received for his culinary work. But it meant a lot to him. In a later interview he explained, "Without question," he told *Georgia Magazine* in 2008, "this is the most gratifying thing in my career. It means the show's not just ok but that it has value and importance, that it says something that needs to be said."

In addition to the Peabody Award, Alton has been recognized many times for the quality of his educational programs about food.

CHAPTER TWO

FROM COAST TO COAST

Alton Brown did not plan on a job working with food. A self-professed movie fanatic, he set his sights at an early age on a career in filmmaking. And for the better part of a decade he followed that career path. But he would ultimately find success by working in the worlds of both food and cinema.

FROM CALIFORNIA TO GEORGIA

Alton Crawford Brown, Jr., was born in Los Angeles, California, on July 30, 1962, to Alton and Phyllis Brown. His parents were from rural Georgia, but they had moved to California shortly before Alton was born.

Alton has described both his parents as being extraordinary. "My mom was a charming woman," he told *Atlanta Magazine*, "who changed the air pressure of a room when she walked into it. My father was a mini-media mogul. And a workaholic, definitely."

Alton spent the first seven years of his life in southern California. Then his parents decided to move back to their home state of Georgia. Alton, Sr., had purchased a small radio station in the town of Cleveland, about 80 miles northeast of Atlanta. The move to White County, in northern Georgia, began with a memorable trip east during the summer of 1969.

Together with the family's Siamese cat, the Browns piled into the family Chrysler sedan and headed east. Their possessions were loaded into a couple of U-Hauls that were driven by friends of the family.

Alton's parents were not interested in taking the fastest way back. Instead, they wanted the trip to be a learning experience that their son would remember. So the family traveled the smaller state and county roads, sampling the food at local restaurants along the way. Alton later wrote:

> We drove and drove and when we got hungry we stopped—never at a chain restaurant but at one of those roadside places with a hand-painted sign in the window and homemade pies under glass. Or maybe a chrome-and-tile luncheonette attached to a gas station with a real Mom and Pop running it. And everywhere we went folks bent over backward to make sure we were treated well—real hospitality, as inviting as the delicious food that they were so eager and proud to serve us.

After having been raised on tacos, enchiladas, guacamole, and other fare common to southern California, Alton discovered an array of new culinary delights as the Brown family traveled through the South, such as blue cheese, barbecued meats, and grits. In addition to experiencing new foods, he was awed by the majestic grandeur of the American landscape the family traveled through. He explained:

> I saw scenery that I thought only existed on jigsaw puzzles. Snow-topped mountains, brilliant desert sunsets, flat prairies with huge white clouds rolling above like tumbleweeds. When we came closer to Georgia the world seemed so green I couldn't believe there weren't sprinklers out there making everything grow. I was a visual kid and those sights are probably what influenced me toward my original career path. . . . But food was always on my mind, as was that magical cross-country journey my family took.

ALTON BROWN, SR.

The family settled in Cleveland, where in 1970 Alton's father purchased the local newspaper, the *White County News*. As its publisher and managing editor, Alton Brown Sr., would use the newspaper as his forum to promote environmental issues. Among other things, his editorials urged the community to establish a sanitary landfill, and he published photos of roadside areas in need of cleaning up.

But when Alton was just 10 years old, his 38-year-old father died. The death was ruled a suicide, although some people questioned that conclusion. A letter printed in the June 28, 1973, edition of the *White County News* noted, "Though Al Brown's untimely death may never be explained and those responsible never brought to justice, through circumstances beyond the control of ordinary citizens, those of us who loved him know he did not live in vain."

Alton was deeply affected by his father's death. "Being a male in this world and growing up without a father to guide you is extraordinarily difficult," he told a journalist with *Atlanta Magazine.* "I think a lot of the mistakes I made along the way have been indirectly the result of being fatherless."

Alton's mother eventually remarried. Alton went from being an only child to a member of a family with a stepfather and stepsiblings.

LEARNING HIS LESSONS

From the time he was a young boy, Alton spent a lot of time cooking in the kitchen with his mother and grandmother, and he credits them with inspiring his interest in the culinary arts. Alton has said that one of his earliest memories was watching his grandmother, Mae Parsons Skelton, prepare his favorite biscuits. Alton described "Ma Mae" on his website:

> Ma Mae wasn't a great cook . . . The highlight of her culinary library was a paperback published by the electric company in 1947. Her oven cooked a hundred degrees hot. She didn't even own a decent knife. And yet, her food was the epitome of good eats. Her chicken and dumplings, greens and cornbread were without equals. Her cobblers were definitive. Her biscuits . . . the stuff of legend.

In the mid-1970s Alton attended Lithonia High School, in the Atlanta suburb of Lithonia. He wrote, "As a youth I was classic bully fodder (fat, slow, nerdy, uncool)." He would later say that as a teen he enjoyed watching movies, ranking science fiction films high among his favorites.

During this time Alton's stepfather encouraged Brown to nurture his interest in food. Alton has said that his stepfather often stated that there were two things that a man needed to know how to do. One was to build things with wood. The other was to cook. Alton heeded the advice. While in high school he took on his first job in the food industry, clearing tables as a busboy at a Hickory House Restaurant near Stone Mountain. He eventually worked his way up to deep-frying chicken. During his high school and college years, he would work at an array of restaurants, ranging from rib shacks to pizza parlors. Despite his restaurant experience, he says, he never seriously considered a career in the culinary field. He was more interested in the cinema.

Although Alton had some academic troubles, he managed to graduate from Lithonia High School in 1980. "Truth is," he told *Macworld* magazine, "I was a horrible student. I sucked at everything because nothing mattered to me. History was a bunch of numbers, chemistry was a bunch of symbols, math was a bunch of equations."

Another issue may have been a need for glasses. It was not until Brown went to college that he learned he was myopic (nearsighted) and had a severe astigmatism (a defect in the lens that distorts how the eye focuses light). Brown told *20/20* magazine, "I'd like to think [poor vision] explains my horrible grades in high school. I never had an eye check up before that."

Brown introduced Ma Mae to viewers on his show *Good Eats* during its first season. In the episode "The Dough Also Rises," which first aired in 1999, he and his grandmother held a friendly biscuit-baking competition. She died in December 2001.

HIGHER EDUCATION

Alton enrolled in LaGrange College in LaGrange, Georgia, to study business. It was around that time that he started wearing glasses. But they didn't help him with his grades. After realizing that he was not cut out for business, he transferred to the University of Georgia (UGA), in Athens, and changed his field of study to filmmaking and theater.

At the university Alton studied under a drama professor named Charley Eidsvik. He would become a big influence. Eidsvik took Brown under his wing and taught him everything he knew about filmmaking. In turn, the professor was impressed by the creativity of his student. "It was an

This historic cast-iron gateway, known as The Arch, stands at the entrance to the University of Georgia's North Campus. Alton attended the university from 1981 to 1985.

extremely lean time in terms of resources," Eidsvik told a reporter with *Georgia Magazine*. "We were working with a shoestring budget. But the beauty of that was that we continually kept inventing. It came naturally to Alton."

GETTING DATES

Alton also honed his culinary skills while at the university. He has often told people that girls who wouldn't usually accept dates from someone like him would agree to go out when he offered them a home-cooked meal. "Yeah," Alton once said, "cooking in college was the only way I got dates. Pathetic, but true."

But Brown would also tell people that he learned an important fact about himself when one girl cancelled on him while he was in the middle of cooking for their date. Rather than stopping, he continued to make the meal. He would later say that he felt committed to finish. He had discovered cooking was fun, even without the girl.

IMPORTANCE OF FOOD

Alton became a "foodie" when he was 21. During the summer of 1983, he spent a couple months performing summer stock in a region of Italy called Tuscany. One day, he was dining at a restaurant in the small town of Cortona. The establishment served only pizza, but every day the owner made a different kind, depending on his mood and the foods that were available.

Impressed that the pizza was unlike any he had ever had, Alton had a revelation. "It was the cultural significance of food," he explained. "Its real power is connecting people to people. I was 21, watching a household with four generations living under one roof, and the way food was prepared tied it all together. Food has a valuable place in culture and the importance that people put on even the simplest things."

A Career in Cinematography

Although Alton considered cooking a favorite hobby, when he looked for a job, he did not seek work in the food industry. In 1985 he left the University of Georgia without obtaining his degree. He was just one credit hour short of the graduation requirement, but he was ready to move on. (Brown would obtain a degree in drama from UGA nearly two decades later, in 2004, after the school changed graduation requirements and no longer required the foreign language credit that he lacked.)

In the years that followed Alton found work as a cameraman with local production companies. Eventually he was also directing commercials and corporate films. In 1987 Brown served as director of photography for the music video, "The One I Love," by the Athens-based rock band R.E.M. He also served as the Steadicam operator in filming the 1988 movie *School Daze*, directed by Spike Lee. (A Steadicam is a stabilizing mount for cameras. It is attached to the cameraman by a mechanical harness and allows for smooth handheld shots despite movement by the operator.)

Personal Life

Alton had married right after leaving college, but his career as a cameraman and cinematographer lasted longer than the marriage. He would later acknowledge that the union was a mistake. "I understand now that love is a verb," he told *Atlanta Magazine*. "It's nothing that happens to you; it's got absolutely nothing to do with romance. It's the action of commitment and the values that come out of that." After a brief marriage, Alton and his wife divorced.

Brown's next marriage would be much stronger. In the early 1990s, while working as a director at a television commercial production firm, he met his second wife. DeAnna Collins was a production manager with the company. The attraction between the two was immediate and they soon married, forming what would prove to be both a valuable personal and professional partnership.

AN IDEA TAKES HOLD

Alton continued working as a cameraman and directing television commercials. But although he was successful, he was not happy. "I really did not like hiring myself out to work on advertising projects very much," he told *Channel Guide Magazine*. "I didn't think it was very worthwhile. The world's got enough Pampers and retread tires and whatnot without me."

When he was not working, Brown spent a lot of his time watching cooking shows on television. A favorite was *The*

GORDON WILLIS

One of Alton's favorite cinematographers is Gordon Willis. He is best known for his work on the *Godfather* movies, as well as for the Woody Allen films *Annie Hall*, *Manhattan*, *Stardust Memories*, *Zelig*, *Broadway Danny Rose*, and *The Purple Rose of Cairo*.

Many people consider Willis to be one of the most influential cinematographers in history. He is known for his deftness in using shadow and underexposed film to create sepia tones such as those seen in *The Godfather: Part II*. Another of his trademarks is a preference for filming just before twilight in order to take advantage of the colors offered by the setting sun.

Frugal Gourmet, starring Jeff Smith. Brown told the *Wall Street Journal* that he was a great fan of Smith. "When his television show, 'The Frugal Gourmet,' made its debut on PBS in the 1980s," Alton said, "it conveyed such genuine enthusiasm for cooking that I was moved for the first time to slap down cold cash for a collection of recipes. Since it was my only cookbook at the time . . . I made every recipe in it, several times."

But Alton had a low opinion of most other cooking programs. He found them repetitive and not very interesting. "Nobody was giving us any explanation," he explained in an interview. "I complained to my wife about the fact that all these shows were boring and dull and she finally got tired of hearing me complain about it and said, 'Well, why don't you do something about it?' and I said, 'Fine, I will.'"

In order to produce the kind of cooking show that Alton had in mind, he needed a better background in the culinary arts than what he had picked up from his mother and grandmother. Doing additional research was not enough. He would have to go to a cooking school.

Alton and DeAnna decided that he would apply to three top-tier cooking schools, and if he got accepted at one, they would sell their house in Atlanta. While Alton attended classes, DeAnna would continue to work to support them.

In 1995 the New England Culinary Institute in Montpelier, Vermont, accepted Alton. He and DeAnna quit their jobs, sold their house, gathered their belongings, and moved north.

In 2000 Brown would pay homage to Jeff Smith's *The Frugal Gourmet* by titling a *Good Eats* episode "The Fungal Gourmet."

CHAPTER THREE

A DIFFERENT KIND OF SHOW

Located in the Green Mountains of Vermont, the New England Culinary Institute was founded in 1980 by Fran Voigt and John Dranow. Its first graduating class consisted of just seven chefs. Fifteen years later, when Alton began his studies there, the school had established itself as one of the country's top culinary schools.

THE NEW ENGLAND CULINARY INSTITUTE

Alton enrolled in NECI in 1995. While he attended classes, DeAnna worked in the school's public relations department. Making ends meet was difficult. Alton's decision to attend the two-year cooking school program made a serious dent in their finances. He later admitted, "We went from making a pretty decent income in Atlanta, with a house and a pool, to living in a third-floor walk-up on $22,000 a year. . . . Those were not glamorous years. And there were plenty of times where [DeAnna] was the only one that believed that it was still possible. Because I lost the faith many times along the way."

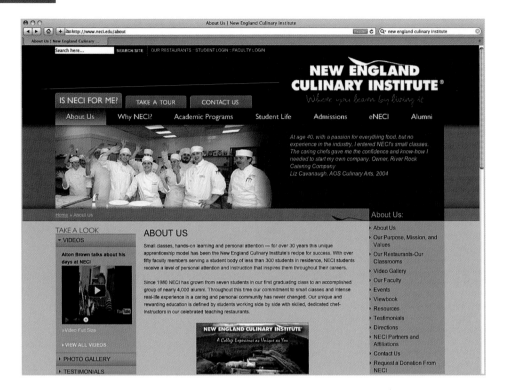

Today, the website of the New England Culinary Institute features a video of Alton talking about his experiences at the school.

Alton was attending NECI to get the background necessary for him to develop a new type of television cooking program. The other students, who envisioned careers as chefs, thought he was crazy. Rather than encouraging him, they teased and taunted him, saying he would never make a cooking program, but would wind up working at McDonald's.

Determined to prove them wrong, Brown applied himself to his studies. Although he had not been interested in science in high school or college, he thrived on learning about the subject in culinary school. "When I started learning how to cook and started studying food," he told the *St. Petersburg Times*, "I started finding that all that science actually means something. . . . I find that the way I can control my food and have knowledge and power over my food is to understand the science of why things happen."

Instead of asking about cooking techniques and recipes, Alton pestered his instructors with questions about why various cooking processes had the effects they did. His teachers would get annoyed or ignore him because they either did not know the answers, or did not think it was necessary to know such information in order to become a successful cook. Alton would later say that most chefs basically understand the science behind what they are doing. However, many of them cannot easily explain these principles to others. Being a good chef does not automatically make someone a good teacher.

To get answers Alton turned to research journals and books at the public library. However, the book that proved most helpful to him was one he received from DeAnna. She gave him a copy of *On Food and Cooking: The Science and Lore of the Kitchen*, published in 1984 by science writer Harold McGee. Alton told *Chemical and Engineering News*, "The one book that changed my life was the first edition of 'On Food and Cooking.' When I was at NECI asking these burning questions, my wife gave me a copy for my birthday and it was like the floodgates opening. It was the one place where I could find an answer that I could understand."

On Food and Cooking: The Science and Lore of the Kitchen was a 680-page book published in 1984. Twenty years later Harold McGee published a revised, updated edition. The 896-page book was honored in 2011 by being included in the James Beard Foundation Cookbook Hall of Fame.

Since 2006, food science writer Harold McGee has written "The Curious Cook," a regular column that appears in the *New York Times*. In it he explores scientific research on food, cooking, and eating.

JEAN-PATRICK MATECAT

A major part of NECI instruction is giving students hands-on experience working in commercial kitchens. Being an intern at age 34 was not easy, Alton admitted later. He told *Channel Guide*, "The internships that I did—going from being a commercial director where, you know, you were The Guy, to being nobody—'Here's the broom; sweep the walk-in'—was extremely humbling. . . . But I'm sure glad I did it. Learned a lot about myself."

Alton has said that one of his most valuable internships was with a French chef named Jean-Patrick Matecat. He worked as executive chef at a restaurant called The Common Man, located in Warren, Vermont. Matecat was a severe taskmaster, and he had the demeanor of a drill sergeant. Alton would later say that he was afraid of the chef at first. But he persevered. Week after week, he worked hard to prove himself and eventually he earned the chef's respect.

Matecat ultimately taught Brown things he had never thought about before. He explained, "[Matecat] understood that to be a chef, you actually have to start by knowing how to eat and I didn't. . . . This guy taught me from the ground up." By the time Alton left the internship, he says, he considered Matecat a father figure. In a 2002 interview Alton called him the chef he most respected and admired. He readily acknowledged that the French master chef made Brown not only a better chef, but a better person as well.

PURSUING THE DREAM

After graduating from NECI in 1997, Alton worked at a series of restaurants to get more "real world" experience. He never, however, worked as a chef. "I did my time in kitchens," he said in an interview with *A.V. Club*, "but I never worked a higher level than lead cook. It's very much a young person's game. Let's just say chefs have a very high rate of alcoholism, divorce, and suicide, and I am not interested in any of those things."

What Brown was interested in was producing a new kind of cooking show—one that was different from all the other dull, boring cooking shows on television. "All at once I could

THE COMMON MAN

The restaurant in Warren, Vermont, where Alton served his internship under head chef Jean-Patrick Matecat was originally called Orsini's La Pasta. When former diamond miner Mike Ware bought the restaurant in 1972, he renamed it The Common Man. The dining establishment earned a reputation as one of the best in the state, where it became known for serving consistently good European fare.

The Common Man was so well known that in 1987, when the 19th-century barn that housed the restaurant burned to the ground, the devastating fire made the front page of *USA Today*. Ware replaced the lost building with an 1854 barn that he had moved to the original site and renovated to recreate the original restaurant. Located in north central Vermont, The Common Man is near the mountain resorts of Sugarbush and Mad River Glen.

see it from behind the lens," he wrote, "could picture it, but I didn't just want to shoot it. I wanted to be in it. I wanted to find a way to communicate the excitement, the passion, the pleasure I first experienced with food on that childhood journey."

Alton wanted to make a food program that would educate and entertain at the same time, and he had some very specific ideas about how to do that. He would later say that the resulting program was part Julia Child, part Monty Python, and part Mr. Wizard. Julia Child was a cooking legend who in the 1960s debuted television's first popular cooking program. Monty Python was a British comedy group whose quirky television show became a cult favorite in the 1970s in both England and the United States. And Mr. Wizard was the name of a character played by Don Herbert, who hosted a popular kids' show in the 1950s and an updated version for cable television in the 1980s. Mr. Wizard taught basic principles of science through entertaining laboratory experiments.

Alton was working the grill at a restaurant in Durham, North Carolina, when he began writing a script for his show. DeAnna suggested a title and *Good Eats* was born.

Alton envisioned a program in which each episode focused on one food. He chose steak as the subject for one

In 2010 Alton Brown delivered the commencement address at UGA's spring graduation ceremony. The following year he served as commencement speaker at the 2011 graduation ceremony at the New England Culinary Institute.

Mr. Wizard (Don Herbert) conducts an experiment with a pair of teenagers in this scene from a 1971 episode of the popular television show. Alton watched Mr. Wizard as a child, and wanted his own cooking show to educate viewers in a similar way.

pilot episode and potatoes for the other. Utilizing his love of puns, he titled the episodes "Steak Your Claim" and "This Spud's for You."

PILOT EPISODES

After completing the writing in 1997, Alton filmed the two pilot episodes with his friends at an Atlanta film company. They agreed to fund the episodes with one stipulation—Alton had to be the host, since they could not afford to hire one. He would later say that the idea had made him nervous at first. Having spent the better part of the previous decade

In an interview, Alton explained how he chose the foods for the first two episodes of Good Eats. *"I chose steak for our first episode for two simple reasons. First, it's the uncontested quintessential American meal—an honest, straightforward, plain-talking promise of plenty. Steak is an edible Copland symphony, and to eat one is to converse with the ghost of John Wayne," he said. "I also chose steak because I wanted* Good Eats *to be a show about the actual processes of cooking. From that standpoint, steak is perfect. . . . If you're making two pilots for a new food show and the first is about steak, you really don't have to think too hard about what the next subject should be: potatoes.*

behind a camera rather than in front of one, he had planned on serving as the program's writer and director—not its host. He finally agreed, however, and the two pilots were completed by the end of 1997.

It took over a year to sell the show. To help make ends meet in the Brown household, Alton catered and taught cooking classes. In July 1998 he managed to get the episodes aired on the Chicago, Illinois, Public Broadcasting Service

(PBS) station WTTW-TV. He told *Macworld*, "We kind of agreed to trade them: They could use the pilots if they would pay for Nielsen ratings for the shows. So they aired those two initial pilots several times, and the numbers were pretty astounding, incredibly astounding." The Nielsen ratings are the system used by Nielsen Media Research to determine the number of viewers watching a particular show and their composition.

The pilot episodes of *Good Eats* also received good reviews in Chicago newspapers. *Chicago Tribune* television critic Steve Johnson raved about the show, saying:

> [T]his PBS series attempts to be a cooking show inspired more by MTV than Julia Child. Mostly it succeeds, as writer-host Alton Brown dares vacate the kitchen to actually visit spots where cows are raised, meat thermometers are sold, etc. The spiky, energetic camera work is first rate, the episodes are shot on luxurious film, and Brown's writing and on-camera presence are sharp enough to hold up to the aggressive production. . . . This lively, well made and refreshingly different show deserves a place at a television table overcrowded with cookie-cutter cooking programs.

Brown worked to sell the show to a specialty cable television channel. He almost had a deal with the Discovery Channel, but he did not like the terms. He believed that a more appropriate home would be the Food Network.

THE FOOD NETWORK

The Food Network was one of the early cable specialty channels. It was the brainchild of Reese Schonfeld, one of the founders of the Cable News Network (CNN). Originally known as the TV Food Network, it began airing programs on April 19, 1993. Among the first shows were *Essence of Emeril, Taste, Pick of the Day*, and *How to Boil Water*. In 1994 it acquired the rights to some of the early, classic Julia Child episodes, which became part of the network's lineup.

The network's popularity grew quickly. By 1998 some of the hosts of its programs, such as chefs Emeril Lagasse, Mario Batali, and Bobby Flay, had attained celebrity status and become household names.

Alton had visions of *Good Eats* being added to the Food Network's programming schedule. But in 1998 the network was producing its own shows. Brown had no contacts at the Food Network and couldn't get anyone to look at the *Good Eats* pilot episodes.

In the meantime, the Eastman Kodak Company, which produces photographic materials and equipment, was featuring some clips of the *Good Eats* pilot episodes on its website. The episodes had been shot on 16-mm Kodak film. Alton explained, "They liked the process I used, and wanted to show off what the particular Kodak film I used could do. It seemed so ironic. But I was proud of my work and glad that at least one minute of it could be seen."

By chance, a Food Network programming executive named Matthew Stillman saw the clips. He liked the idea of the show and set up a meeting. Within a month, Brown had a deal. The Food Network bought the rights to *Good Eats*, and it premiered on July 7, 1999. *Good Eats* became the Food Network's first commissioned show.

A few months after *Good Eats* debuted, another Alton Brown production made a first appearance. Daughter Zoey was born to Alton and DeAnna in January 2000.

CHAPTER FOUR

ANATOMY OF A HIT

Alton wanted *Good Eats* to be different from other cooking shows. He didn't want to just present recipes; he wanted the viewer to learn. To hold viewers' interest, he incorporated various forms of comedy, including word play and slapstick. To bring home a point, he was not above having crewmembers impersonate Elvis Presley or dress like an onion.

PREPARATION AND RESEARCH

Deciding on a topic for an episode of *Good Eats* was not simply a matter of selecting a particular food. Brown preferred to place emphasis on cooking techniques rather than recipes. In 2002 he told an interviewer, "I'll come up with a list of procedures, things that are basic lessons or basic applications. And sometimes it will start with an application—stir frying or controlling a grill—and then finding foods that are really good examples of how to have that control."

After determining the subject of an episode, Brown would then list the major points that he wanted to make in that show. He typically would communicate these concepts by using comedy, props, and bits and pieces of pop culture. Brown typically provided much of the pop culture trivia used in the show. He has often compared himself to a big piece of Velcro that rolls along picking up interesting bits and pieces of movie, television, music, and cultural information.

WRITING THE SCRIPT

Next came writing the script, which required a tremendous amount of research in books, periodicals, journals, interviews, and the Internet. In June 2001 Alton told the *Atlanta Journal and Constitution*, "My show is heavily researched—we gather 2,000 to 3,000 pages of research a year."

The research and writing was done using an Apple computer. Brown got his first computer in 1991 and quickly became addicted to the technology. "I kind of quickly moved through a successive line of computers," he told *MacWorld* in 2001, "and I can't imagine now doing any of what I do without them. It's just inconceivable to me."

Alton soon became dependent on Apple computers because of the editing software. "You've got certain tools that you have to have," he explained, "and so you're very, very picky; and once you make up your mind about what you're going to go with, you stick with it. . . . I have definitely become that way with Macintoshes. And I do not think that I could do what I do without them."

In 2003, beginning with season seven, Brown began to leave some of the research and writing to Rob DeBorde. Due to restrictions on his time he no longer did all the research and writing for *Good Eats*. But making that move was difficult, he told *Channel Guide*. "It took me a long time to find someone with the same background and whatnot and I finally found him. But boy, it hurts," he said. "It's really, really difficult for me because it feels as if I am losing ownership."

PRODUCTION AND THE SET

Before full-scale production of an episode could begin, preproduction tasks needed to be completed. These included gathering together actors, props, cooking supplies and gadgets, and any special equipment.

Alton takes a closer look at salsa and chips during an episode of Good Eats.

Next, the actual filming of scenes took place. Episodes were filmed on the kitchen set as well as at various locations. DeAnna served as one of the show's producers for seasons one and two. She and Alton partnered with The Means Street Productions, which produced the first four seasons of *Good Eats*. These shows aired between July 1999 and October 2001. During that time the kitchen of a home in Atlanta was used for the set.

Alton prepares a demonstration in the original Good Eats *kitchen. The paper maché chicken in the background was a gift from Alton's mother.*

In 2001 Alton formed his own production company, with DeAnna serving as its head. They called the new company Be Square Productions, and it assumed production of the show beginning with season five.

Filming took place in the kitchen of the show's line producer, Dana Popoff, and her husband, Marion Laney, the *Good Eats* director of photography. When they purchased the home, they planned that the kitchen would be used as a television studio. In 2003 Dana told *Home Magazine*, "Our first requirement was that we wanted several areas to shoot in. We wanted a sitting area and a fireplace that would be separate, but could also be part of the kitchen. We also liked the idea of a banquette, and we wanted to make the whole space as open as possible so we could move around and have a variety of backgrounds."

In order to help with varying camera angles, part of the work island was built on wheels. In this way, it could be relocated when and where it was needed. The one broadcasting necessity that seemed out of place in a private home was the grid of pipes suspended from the ceiling. They were needed for attaching lights and microphones during shootings.

Popoff and Laney's home was used for only seasons five and six. Neighbors in the area complained that shooting the television show created problems. Rather than incur the wrath of the community, Be Square moved production to a facility in Atlanta. An exact duplicate of the kitchen was built on a sound stage.

After filming was completed and an episode's scenes recorded, they were edited and then sent to the sound designer, Patrick Belden. Belden would add music, voiceovers, and sound effects. Once the audio was complete, all of the components were ready for final assembly and the insertion of graphics. These visuals typically included slides, recipes, and text pieces such as the trivia sidebars shown before commercial breaks.

Both Alton and Food Network staff would do a final review of each episode to check for errors or other glitches. Taking control of—and being responsible for—production through his own company gave Alton the opportunity to make improvements to the show. In 2002 he said, "We've made changes to the way the video actually works, technical stuff," Alton told an interviewer. "Post-production is a lot slicker. The shows are cleaner. They flow better. There was a lot of very, kind of, rough editorial things that happened in the first three to four seasons. Now there's a lot more flow."

THE CAST AND CREW

The cast of *Good Eats* included several recurring characters, both real and fictional. The real ones include a cookbook author (Shirley Corriher), a nutritional anthropologist

THE *GOOD EATS* THEME

Patrick Belden of Belden Music and Sound served as audio engineer for *Good Eats*. Alton and Belden had worked together on several projects for Jayan Films in the early 1990s. After graduating from NECI in 1995, Alton called on Belden to help with *Good Eats*.

Belden has credited the original 10-note theme written for the pilot episodes to Atlanta composer, Nikki Saxxs. As of 2000, Belden said, he had used more than 70 different instruments to play the *Good Eats* theme. He also produced all of the other snippets of music that occur through the show—as well as the post-production sound for *Good Eats*.

(Deborah Duchon), a nutritionist (Caroline Connell), and a dietitian (Carolyn O'Neil). Other real-life people to appear in various episodes have included Alton's grandmother, mother, and daughter.

Actors who played characters on the shows were sometimes referred to as the Good Eats Players. One of the most well known was Vickie Eng, who played the kitchen gear specialist known as "W"—a spoof of the Q character from James Bond films. In real life, Eng is actually Alton's chiropractor. Many other characters—both recurring and one-time—were played by members of the crew. At some time or other, all of the show's staff members appeared on camera.

Once A-Pun a Time

Comedy in all its forms was a vital part of *Good Eats*. It influenced the title of each episode, which usually consisted of puns or plays on words. For example, the "Long Arm of the Slaw," featured slaw, or shredded cabbage; "Casserole Over" covered casseroles; and "Ill Gotten Grains" discussed wheat grains. Some titles were inspired by movies: "Fruit Ten from Outer Space" featured the pomegranate and "Honey I Shrunk the Cake" highlighted cupcakes.

Other episode names came from television: "Chile's Angels" focused on chile peppers and "Mission: Poachable" on poaching fish. Word play was inspired by the names of musicals (*The King and I* became "The Wing and I," for a show on buffalo wings) and literature (for a segment on crepes, *Great Expectations* became "Crepe Expectations," and dried fruit changed *Wuthering Heights* into "Withering Bites"). Popular music also provided inspiration as "Puff the Magic Dragon" evolved into "Puff the Magic Pastry," and "Wake Up Little Susie" became "Wake Up Little Sushi."

One of the most challenging parts of putting together the show, Alton said, was effectively combining humor with learning. In 2002 he told an interviewer, "Comedy is real hard. When the comedy works, that's very satisfying because comedy is very elusive. Sometimes on paper what's funny doesn't translate. When those things really come together, that's what makes it really fun to shoot."

Alton worked to incorporate all forms of humor in *Good Eats*. "Highbrow, lowbrow, I don't think in those terms," he said. "I think things are either funny or they're not funny. There are things that are going to be funny to an eight-year old and I want that there because I'm still an eight-year old in a lot of my brain."

Comedy on *Good Eats* also inspired the show's props. *Good Eats* made extensive use of props that ranged from a six-foot-tall human nose, used in "Fruit 10 from Outer Space," to a giant kernel of popcorn that appeared in "Pop Art."

In 2002 Alton was quick to praise the people responsible for putting the show together. "I have the best people in the world," he said. "That's the biggest satisfaction of any of this . . . the people that I work with. They're unparalleled. How I have managed through my years of working in commercial production and movie production to amass the level of people that I have, I don't deserve them . . . I'm the catalyst for great people, and they are. Every department is remarkable. Really remarkable."

A NEW KITCHEN

Around 2005 Be Square Productions moved again, this time to a new 15,000 square-foot studio complex housed in an industrial park. *Good Eats* has a distinct visual style, and the kitchen set had been custom built for filming shots from

Viewers were allowed a glimpse of the *Good Eats* creation process in the episode "Behind the Eats," which first aired in July 2006.

inside the oven, refrigerator, or microwave. For many years the *Good Eats* crew used tape and other adhesives to place cameras inside of appliances—and at least one camera melted in the oven. The new set contained appliances, cabinets, and walls with areas cut out that would allow for easy filming.

Be Square first used the set for filming season nine. In addition to the *Good Eats* kitchen set, the new production facility featured fully functional test kitchens, editing suites, a sound booth, and a research library. Among the items reported in 2007 to be decorating the space were huge vegetable props, a life-sized fiberglass cow, and a giant popcorn kernel.

In 2005 Alton's home at the time, in Marietta, Georgia, was shown on the program. It took center stage when season nine's "Give Peas a Chance" was aired that June. It can also be seen in the Food Network's *All Star Thanksgiving Special*. Grilling scenes were also occasionally shot in the backyard.

CABLE IN THE CLASSROOM

The Food Network quickly identified *Good Eats* as an appealing program for teaching kids about food science, nutrition, and health, and the network made the program available to *Cable in the Classroom*, an educational outreach effort of the U.S. cable industry. It encourages the innovative use of technology and media in private homes, schools, and communities across the country.

In January 2001, as part of the *Cable in the Classroom* program, the Food Network began airing commercial-free *Good Eats* videos that could be recorded for educational use. Accompanying lesson plans and teacher's guides were also provided, courtesy of the Food Network and Alton Brown. These lessons and activities connected the show's content to school subjects such as science, nutrition, and health. As a result, *Good Eats* soon gained a sizable following among grade-school age kids.

SUCCESS

Good Eats proved to be a huge success, attracting a dedicated following among viewers of all ages, male and female. It soon became one of Food Network's top rated shows, drawing more than 20 million viewers a month.

In September 2004 Brown was named "Cooking Teacher of the Year" by *Bon Appétit* magazine. It noted in its October 2004 issue "Alton Brown . . . transformed his love of food (and frustration with dull cooking shows) into a career devoted to demystifying the way we cook. . . . Brown is fast becoming a trusted kitchen companion."

The show brought Alton fame as a television personality. In 2006 the Food Network built on that fame by basing an advertising campaign on him. Brown's face appeared on billboards. Television ads for *Good Eats* ran on several different cable channels. And print ads played up Alton's expertise in food science by featuring such images as atoms made out of spaghetti and meatballs.

CHAPTER FIVE

AUTHOR AND SPOKESMAN

Alton's success on *Good Eats* provided new opportunities. Among them was the chance to publish books and to work with several outside companies, as both a spokesman and a consultant.

FOOD PLUS HEAT

Brown published his first cookbook in May 2002. He completed the manuscript in just three months, he says, by following an extreme writing regimen. He explained in an interview, "I literally locked myself in a 28-foot Airstream trailer for three months," he said, "and day after day, I forced myself to write for four hours and then sleep for two. I remember not knowing if it was day or night. . . . When I was done, I thought the book was horrible. I was so ashamed of it."

The result of his efforts, *I'm Just Here for the Food: Food + Heat = Cooking*, is more than a collection of recipes. It is an expression of Alton's philosophy of cooking. Cooking, by definition, means preparing food for eating by applying heat.

The book explores the different methods of doing this. Brown wanted to show the reader the importance of applying the correct amount of heat when cooking. In this way, the reader would better understand how to control the cooking process and thereby produce better food.

Instead of being arranged by the course or ingredient, the book is categorized by cooking method. The focus is on explaining why certain processes occur so that the reader can apply that knowledge rather than just follow a recipe. The book does feature recipes. They, the original graphics, and Alton's wacky sense of humor come together to illustrate specific points.

Although Alton may have had doubts about the quality of his work, the critics did not. A reviewer for *Publishers Weekly* praised the book, saying:

> Alton Brown brings an MTV style to food and cooking. He applies his winning formula of pop culture combined with history, science and common sense to his first cookbook. . . . Despite its unconventional style, this is a solid volume presented in a lively, fun manner guaranteed to put cooking in the reach of just about anyone: Alton Brown + Cook = Success.

I'm Just Here for the Food was a great success. Editors and readers at Amazon.com selected it as one of the top 50 books of the year for 2002. In 2003 it won the James Beard Foundation Award for Best Cookbook in the Reference category. The prestigious award was both surprising and humbling to Alton. "I don't have a restaurant," he said. "I don't wear white chef's coats anymore. I'm kind of an outsider. Having the hard-core food community say 'you're OK' . . . well, I don't think I deserved it, but I'm not giving it back."

That same year Alton told the *Austin Chronicle*, "I love cooking because the kitchen is a great place to play. And the fact that I can feed people is a great side-benefit. See, I love playing with fire. My book may be called *I'm Just Here for the Food*, but I'm really just here to play."

TOOLS AND GADGETS

That interest in playing with food includes exploring the various tools and gadgets used in the kitchen. On *Good Eats* Alton typically looked for ways to make things easier to do, and to find new uses for the tools that he already had. He ventured the opinion that many cooking implements were no

Alton discusses oysters as he opens one with a kitchen knife on Good Eats.

more than glorified items that could be found in any hardware store. His goal, he said, was to have fewer things in his kitchen, and to find new uses for tools that no one else had yet discovered.

On *Good Eats*, Alton defined a *unitasker* as a tool with only one function or that was good for only one job. The only unitasker in Alton's kitchen, he proudly proclaimed in several episodes, was a fire extinguisher.

An example of Alton's ingenuity in the kitchen was his using empty tuna fish cans as pastry rings for homemade English muffins and unglazed quarry tiles as pizza stones. He also improvised a device for making beef jerky by using car filters, a bungee cord, and a fan. A favorite quote was one by Theodore Roosevelt: "Do what you can, with what you have, where you are."

Brown would make his point by improvising cooking gadgets on the show rather than using expensive, store-bought ones. For example, on one *Good Eats* episode on smoking salmon, he used a hot plate, cardboard box, cast iron skillet, and sawdust to construct a smoker. This use of kitchen "hacks," as Alton called them, led to the publication of his second book in September 2003, *Alton Brown's Gear for Your Kitchen.*

In the introduction to *Gear for Your Kitchen,* Alton compares himself to MacGyver, the secret agent from the 1980s TV show of the same name. The character was known for his resourcefulness in solving problems by using common everyday items. Brown explains, "Like MacGyver, I get great pleasure from using what I know to concoct cheaper, easier, convenient-er, fun-er ways of cooking. I like the exercise of figuring out new ways to apply tools, to eke more efficiency and usefulness out of every object in my kitchen."

Gear for Your Kitchen is divided into six chapters. Topics covered are Pots and Pans, Sharp Things, Small Things with Plugs, Kitchen Tools Unplugged, Storage and Containment, and Safety and Sanitation. Rather then presenting an encyclopedia of kitchen tools and utensils, Brown helps readers have fun with cooking by showing them how to select the tools that are right for them. In the book he notes that the most expensive tools are not always the best. What is important is that the tools be comfortable to use. Brown also presents a four-step plan for eliminating unnecessary items from the kitchen.

Alton's second book also received many positive reviews. *Publishers Weekly* raved, "Brown has all the colander knowledge, marketing savvy, and geeky male appeal to whip up a big hit from this unwieldy but very fun macropedia of gadgetry." The book was nominated for a James Beard Award in the Best Cookbook in the Tools and Techniques category. It

Alton films one of his shows for the Food Network. His television appearances have given Alton opportunities to earn significant money through cookbook sales and product endorsements.

was also nominated for an International Association of Culinary Professionals (IACP) award in the Food Reference/Technical category.

MIXING PLUS HEAT

In October 2004 Brown brought out a third book. *I'm Just Here for More Food: Food x Mixing + Heat = Baking* followed the basic style of the first book. But rather than dealing with using heat to prepare basic foods such as meat and vegetables, this book concerned itself with the "how" and "why" of baking, giving scientific background on the properties and functions of proteins, carbohydrates, and fats. *I'm Just Here for More Food* also incorporated a new feature. In an interview with *Roadfly* magazine, Alton explained:

> I realized that with baking, you're really only using the same seven or eight ingredients—not a lot changes with each recipe. Rather, it's the mixing technique that leads to variations in the final product, so the book focuses on mixing methods, and with each section, there's a cool 'master flap' that describes the processes. So instead of repeating information over and over within a section, the flap serves as a quick point of reference, and should make it easier to read and follow.

Brown also contributed to the 2005 cookbook *Food Network Favorites: Recipes from Our All-Star Chefs*. Part of the royalties went to the charity group Heifer International. The global nonprofit organization strives to end hunger and poverty by providing livestock and seeds to people living in poverty so they can support themselves. Alton has been a longtime supporter of Heifer International.

MONETARY REWARDS

Good Eats did not bring Alton immediate wealth. When the Food Network picked up the show, Alton Brown was unknown and the network purchased full rights. Despite the fact that its episodes have been shown many times over the years, cable show residuals (the money paid to a performer for a repeat of a television show) are typically not very much.

It was also very expensive to create each episode, Brown has said. The costs of producing *Good Eats* were much higher than those of other cooking shows. The episodes generally had more expenses because they were filmed in various locations, in addition to the kitchen set, and props and other sets had to be built. It also took more time to produce an episode than was needed for other programs on the Food Network. For example, chef Emeril Lagasse could turn out three episodes of his shows in a single day, while it took Brown an average of three days to complete one *Good Eats* episode.

But Alton reaped monetary awards from opportunities that arose as a result of the show. These include speaking engagements, appearances at corporate events, and endorsements. He has said that he is able to make the same amount of money in a single week of corporate work that he made from a full season of *Good Eats*.

Alton receives royalties from *Good Eats* DVD sales. And his book sales also supply him with sizable returns. "I spent three months writing my first book," he told an interviewer in April 2007, "and every six months I go to the mailbox and there's a big fat check. I like the way that works."

KNIVES, GRAPES, AND OVENS

Alton's work for the Food Network, as well as his successful cookbooks, established him as a well-respected food authority. As such, many companies looking to cash in on his name approached him with lucrative offers. But because he refused to endorse a product he did not personally use and believe in, he turned most of them down.

The *Good Eats* policy was to avoid featuring specific products—an advertising practice known as product placement. Even kitchen appliances on the set had their logos removed or covered. However, there were three companies for which Alton agreed to serve as consultant or spokesperson.

In 2003 Alton helped develop a line of knives for Shun Knives. They are known as the Shun Classic Alton Angle series. The knives have blades that sport a 10-degree angle at the bolster—the juncture where the blade meets the handle. This gives the user better leverage on the blade, which can result in a more efficient slicing action. Because the knives are of high quality steel, the blades can be ground to a very fine angle, which gives them an extremely sharp edge. Brown has also produced videos endorsing the knives, which are offered for sale online.

Alton helped General Electric develop a new type of high-technology oven called the Trivection oven.

In 2006 GE hired Alton to teach its engineers how food cooks so they could build better appliances. His consultant work helped in the creation of its Trivection oven, which combines thermal, convection, and microwave technology. To cook something, the user simply enters the food type, time, and temperature, and the oven does the rest. The new technology allows foods to cook as much as five times faster than they would in a conventional oven. Brown says that what he likes most about the Trivection oven is that it balances three different types of energies in order to maximize cooking performance in the kitchen.

Because he feels strongly about the health benefits of grape juice, Alton signed on to endorse Welch's 100 percent grape juice in 2008. In the press release announcing his contract with Welch Foods, Brown praised its beverage product, explaining, "The grape in question

Alton has appeared in ads for Welch's grape juice since 2008.

is of course the Concord, which besides being delicious, and extremely versatile, is great for your health. That's because it's packed with nutrients called polyphenols which appear to help protect healthy cells from the damaging effects of unstable molecules, called free radicals." Alton is part of the company's print campaign and has appeared in several commercials promoting the health benefits of the juice.

A *free radical* is a highly unstable molecule that can chemically combine with oxygen and cause damage to the body. An *antioxidant* is a substance that helps neutralize unstable molecules by inhibiting oxidation.

Alton poses with celebrity chefs Bobby Flay (left) and Michael Symon in "Kitchen Stadium," where the Food Network program Iron Chef America *takes place.*

CHAPTER SIX

FOOD NETWORK STAR

As host of *Good Eats* and the author of several cookbooks, Brown had become a familiar face to many Americans by 2004. So when executives at the Food Network began developing a new cooking show, it was natural that they turned to Alton to serve as host.

IRONMEN OF COOKING

The new show was based on a Japanese program that premiered on the Fuji Television network in October 1992. It was called *Ryori no Tetsujin*, roughly translated as *Ironmen of Cooking*. Unlike most other cooking shows *Ironmen of Cooking* was a competition rather than a demonstration. It was hosted by a fictional character called Chairman Takeshi Kaga, who was portrayed by Japanese actor Shigekatsu Katsuda.

According to the storyline of the show, Kaga was an eccentric millionaire who constructed a magnificent "Kitchen

Stadium" in his castle. In each episode of the show it housed a cooking competition between a visiting master chef and one of Kaga's three "Iron Chefs" from his Gourmet Academy. Each of the Iron Chefs specialized in a different cuisine: Japanese, Chinese, and French. A fourth Iron Chef specializing in Italian cuisine was added later in the series.

In each episode the flamboyant Chairman, attired in distinctive formal wear, introduced a secret "theme ingredient" to the competing chefs. The chefs then had one hour to produce a four- or five-course meal in which each dish featured the secret ingredient. Chairman Kaga signaled the start of each competition with his signature cry of, "Allez cuisine!" or "Go cook!"

As the chefs and their assistants prepared their dishes, an announcer, a commentator, and a floor reporter gave a running commentary of the proceedings. They discussed the preparation of the dishes and the styles of cooking, and gave background information on the foods being used. At the end of the hour, a panel of judges sampled the dishes, which were rated on taste, presentation, and originality. After the scores were tallied, the winner was announced.

The show was a hit in Japan. *Ironmen of Cooking* ran on Japanese television for seven years, concluding in September 1999 after 309 episodes, and a few specials were produced over the next three years. The Food Network acquired the program's broadcast rights and in late 1999 premiered the

The Kitchen Stadium for *Iron Chef America* is located in a huge television studio in New York City's Chelsea Market.

first episode of the series under the name *Iron Chef*. The Japanese program, which was dubbed in English, quickly became a Food Network favorite, especially among college-age viewers.

In December 2001 *Iron Chef* gave rise to a successor. *Iron Chef USA*, hosted by William Shatner, debuted that month on the UPN television network. It was a dismal failure and was off the air after only two episodes. Around three years later, however, a more worthy successor premiered on the Food Network—*Iron Chef America*.

IRON CHEF AMERICA

Iron Chef America was similar to the original program in that it featured the storyline of the Chairman's Kitchen Stadium and the use of the secret ingredient. But the Iron Chefs were new. They included chefs Bobby Flay, Mario Batali, Masaharu Morimoto, Cat Cora, Jose Garces, Michael Symon, and Marc Forgione. As Iron Chefs, they faced off against various challengers.

Martial artist Mark Dacascos played the role of the Chairman—the storyline was that he was the nephew of the original Chairman, Takeshi Kaga. Kevin Brauch served as floor reporter. And Alton Brown, whose job was to provide information as commentator and play-by-play announcer, was given the role of the program's host. A guest panel of judges would determine the winner of each competition.

Filming began in 2004. As a special to introduce the *Iron Chef America* series, the Food Network first taped a miniseries called "Iron Chef America: Battle of the Masters," which would be broadcast the following January. "Battle of the Masters" pitted American chefs Mario Batali, Bobby Flay, and Wolfgang Puck against Masaharu Morimoto and

Hiroyuki Sakai, two of the original Iron Chefs. While on the set, Alton had to be rushed to the hospital. It appeared that stress, fatigue, and dehydration had caused a heart arrhythmia. *Arrhythmia* is a condition in which the heart beats with an irregular or abnormal rhythm.

It turned out that Alton's condition was not serious. After an overnight stay at St. John's Hospital in Santa Monica, California, Brown was released and was able to resume his responsibilities on the show. Alton later had a different explanation for the attack. He blamed the incident on the oyster broth that was in one of the foods he tasted. He has intolerance to oysters, which could explain his body's reaction. Since the incident, he has avoided tasting dishes prepared on the show, except in cases when he has to stand in for the Chairman at the judging table.

As host and commentator of *Iron Chef America,* Alton stands at a station close to the action at the front of the Kitchen Stadium. Next to him are computer screens that allow him to view closeups of the cooking. His location near the competing chefs allows him to speak with—and question—them during the match. In his job as commentator, Brown frequently intermingles witty observations with bits of culinary trivia and food science.

To prepare for the filming of each episode, Alton has to research the secret theme ingredient for that particular competition. The competitors are given a list of five foods ahead of time. They are told that one of the five foods will be the secret ingredient. The Iron Chef and the challenger are also allowed to stock their kitchen pantry with special items to use during the competition. Alton must learn about all these items, too, so that he will be able to recognize and identify them should they be used during the show.

(Top) In each episode of Iron Chef America, a panel of judges determines the winner. Here, Alton poses with the Chairman (Mark Dacascos, back left) and judges Karine Bakhoum, Cady Huffman, John T. Edge, and Nina Griscom. (Bottom) The Chairman gives the signal to begin, as chefs Michael Symon and Anne Burrell (right) prepare to battle Cat Cora and Robert Irvine.

A two-hour *Iron Chef America* episode that featured first lady Michelle Obama and White House executive chef Cristeta Comerford was the highest rated show on cable TV for its time slot (8 to 10 P.M.). The episode drew about 4.6 million viewers when it aired in January 2010 and remains the most-watched Food Network show to date.

Alton's knowledge of the ingredients and fast-paced commentary are major attractions for viewers of the show. Brown told *Channel Guide*, "One of the reasons that I try so hard to have social context, to have 'story' about the ingredients . . . is to try to fill in the gaps and give purpose and meaning to something that people can't taste. I can't describe for you what passion fruit tastes like. . . . So instead, you give it some context by talking about its history and giving it significance that way."

Regular episodes of *Iron Chef America* debuted January 16, 2005. The show was an instant a hit for the Food Network—the first regular episode drew 2.3 million viewers.

The network saw its ratings increase by 40 percent from ratings for the same time period in 2004.

THE NEXT IRON CHEF

The success of *Iron Chef America* led to a spin-off show called *The Next Iron Chef*, which premiered in 2007 with Alton serving as the program host. Each season of the program consists of a competition between chefs battling for the right to be named the next Iron Chef on *Iron Chef America*.

The Next Iron Chef is very different from *Iron Chef America*. In an interview, Brown explained: "*Iron Chef America* is simple. There's an ingredient. There's another chef. And there's sixty minutes. That's simple compared to what *Next Iron Chef* put them through. They've really gotta explore who they are. There was a lot of culinary soul-searching."

Each challenge on *The Next Iron Chef* revolves around a specific theme. In season one, for example, themes included speed, artistry, simplicity, innovation, resourcefulness, and creativity under pressure. "You could compete on *Iron Chef America* three times," Brown said, "and still not be prepared in any way, shape or form for *Next Iron Chef*. Because the challenges on *Next Iron Chef* are very cerebral. They're very philosophical, in fact. It's not just about competing against someone with a clock."

To Alton, his role on *The Next Iron Chef* is clearly defined. In September 2010 he told *Eater National*:

> *The Next Iron Chef* operates on two principles. Number one, respect for the food. Number two, respect for the chef. Nothing is ever about wanting the chef to fail or wanting to see the chef fall down and have a nervous breakdown. . . . What I want to do is make sure that the last chef standing is the right one for this job. I have a real vested interest in *Iron Chef America* being successful and continuing to be successful. I don't want to muddy it up with bad cooks.

VIRTUAL ALTON

In 2008 Brown made an appearance in a video game. That year the computer game company Destineer came out with *Iron Chef America: Supreme Cuisine* for both the Wii and Nintendo DS gaming systems. Other virtual personalities in the game are the Chairman and Iron Chefs Mario Batali, Cat Cora, and Masaharu Morimoto.

A serious-looking Alton is featured in the lower corner of this promotional poster for the second season of The Next Iron Chef.

Cook or Be Cooked!, developed in 2009 by Namco for the Wii gaming system, was the first video cooking game released by the Food Network.

Iron Chef America: Supreme Cuisine allows players to face off against celebrity chefs. The players meet in the Kitchen Stadium, where they battle through a series of culinary challenges. In a timed competition they must complete three to six dishes. The game features 15 theme ingredients and hundreds of dish variations. It also features a chef school where players can practice their skills. And it has a career mode in which players compete against classic chefs before taking on the Iron Chefs.

Throughout each contest, Alton gives his signature witty commentary on the events, throwing in bits of food trivia. On the *Supreme Cuisine* website, Brown states, "I'm very excited to lend my commentary to *Iron Chef America: Supreme Cuisine*. This project is completely different from what I normally get to do and like a great recipe, it's exciting to see the various components come together in a distinctly *Iron Chef America* manner."

Although the game received lukewarm reviews, Alton was generally well received. A reviewer for the video gaming website GameSpot noted, "Alton Brown is the lone bright spot, as his commentary includes some genuinely interesting facts."

Around the same time that he made his virtual appearance, Brown made several guest appearances on television shows. In 2007 he was the guest programmer on Turner Classic Movies. The following year he voiced a character in the "House Fancy" episode of the animated series *SpongeBob*

SquarePants, on Nickelodeon TV. That same year he made an appearance on *Jeopardy!*—delivering clues for the category "*Good Eats* with Alton Brown."

GOOD EATS: THE TRILOGY

When *I'm Just Here for the Food* was published, *Good Eats* had been on the air for several seasons. Alton, however, had vowed he would not consider a book about *Good Eats* until the show had been on the air for 10 years.

In 2009 the show celebrated its 10-year anniversary. That October, *Good Eats: The Early Years* appeared in stores. The book covered the first 80 episodes of the show. It included facts, photos, and recipes (or "applications," as Brown calls them) from each show. In addition to basic information

Alton speaks to contestants during the third season of The Next Iron Chef.

gleaned from the programs, the book included reworked and new recipes. Brown explained in the introduction:

> We've enhanced some dishes, added new flavors, and, yes, we've made a few small repairs based upon input from fans. . . . There are also brand new applications, for dishes we would have included in the shows if we'd been given an hour slot instead of just thirty minutes. There are hundreds of images from the shows and lots of anecdotes.

Good Eats 2: The Middle Years was published the following year. This second volume covered episodes 81 through 164. As with the first book, recipes were reworked and further material added. The book also included a DVD of short subjects originally filmed as material to fill in the gaps between shows. In describing the book Alton told Zap2it, "They're actually some of my favorite pieces from a filmic standpoint. There's one about Sucralose. . . . There's a short about free range chickens. . . . There's one about grog. There's one about cowboy speak in the culinary world. They're kind of crazy, all over the place little bits."

The final book of the *Good Eats* trilogy, entitled *Good Eats 3: The Later Years*, was published in September 2011. Like the first two volumes, the third included an abundance of information and entertainment, with hundreds of drawings and photographs, as well as more than 200 recipes. Picking up where *Good Eats 2* left off, the book covered the topics of episodes 165 through 249.

For his next project, Alton hit the road to produce a multi-part documentary, Feasting on Asphalt, *about the food at small mom-and-pop roadside restaurants.*

CHAPTER SEVEN

THE TRAVELER

With television episodes to film, speaking engagements to attend, and book tours to make, Brown found that the best way to get around was by plane—with him in the pilot's seat. Flying a plane is more than just a hobby to Alton. It is also an important means of transportation that allows him to spend less time in airports and more time with family.

PILOT

Brown learned to fly at the Superior Flight School in Kennesaw, Georgia. In studying for his license, his approach was similar to that of his approach to cooking. Rather than just learning how to fly, he sought out answers to questions not generally covered in basic training manuals. He wanted to understand the basics of weather, airspace, maneuvers and aerodynamics, and how they interact in the flying experience.

After earning his pilot's credentials in June 2008, Alton purchased a six-seat, single-engine Cessna 206 Turbo. He later added a Cessna 414. He spent more than $20,000 to outfit his Cessna 206 with a global positioning system (GPS). But he explained that he does not depend solely on technology to know where he is. "When I fly," he told the website Gizmodo in 2008, "I may have full GPS on the plane, but I got a full set of charts too, and I keep the charts out while I'm flying to make sure I know where I am . . . there could be a catastrophic satellite failure, different things could happen that could make GPS unusable."

MOTORCYCLIST

Flying a plane is not the only way Alton gets around. In 2008 he crisscrossed the United States on a BMW R1200GS motorcycle. The journey combined work on a third show for the Food Network with one of his favorite hobbies—riding motorcycles.

Alton has said that he had been interested in motorcycles since he was a teenager. But his mother did not share his enthusiasm. In fact, she was "deathly afraid of me getting on any motorcycle," he told *Roadfly*, "so I never bought one." Many years later, in 2002, DeAnna insisted that he treat himself—she told him that he needed to buy a motorcycle. Her only stipulation was that it had to be a new—rather than a used—bike. Alton purchased a Suzuki SV650. "One of the great things about riding a motorcycle," he said in the interview, "is that it's a constant exercise in skill management . . . I'm always trying to learn something new and I'm always looking to improve my skill level."

Alton soon became interested in German-engineered bikes, particularly BMW motorcycles. He traded in his SV650 for a slightly used BMW R1100RT, which he said proved to be extremely reliable and great fun to ride. By the

Alton poses with his BMW R1200RT sport tour bike, which he attempted to ride cross-country while filming Feasting on Asphalt *in 2006.*

time he signed on to do a "road trip" documentary for Food Network, he had upgraded to another BMW bike, the BMW R1200RT.

EXPLORING THE OPEN ROAD

A love for traveling the open road was one of the factors that inspired Brown to make a documentary about eating establishments that cater to travelers and offer special regional cuisine. Another factor was his childhood cross-country trip, when his family moved from California to Georgia. He had many fond memories of the journey, and of the places they stopped to eat and the people they met along the way. The kindness and friendliness of strangers made a strong impression that ultimately affected his attitudes towards foods and the entire dining experience. "To this day I believe that the most important food experience you can have, besides eating with your own family, is to break bread with strangers," he wrote in 2008. "There are few—if any—social acts that can provide so positive a spin on human interactions, and if we did more of it, I feel certain there would be a lot less misery and misunderstanding on this planet."

Alton came up with the idea for the documentary. Called *Feasting on Asphalt*, it would feature him traveling across the country to see if the same type of mom-and-pop eateries he visited as a child still existed on the back roads of America. He approached the project with more than a little apprehension. "To tell you the truth," he later wrote, "I was worried that I wouldn't find the small family-run roadside places of my memory. I feared that down-home hospitality had gone the way of hand-shelled peas and homemade pastry dough. Maybe I was taking my film crew on a nostalgic ride to nowhere."

The four rules followed by the crew in filming *Feasting on Asphalt* were simple:

1. Alton and his crew would travel on back roads and avoid the larger interstate highways whenever possible.
2. They would not eat at national chain restaurants but stick to local establishments that served "road food," or food for travelers.
3. There would be no whining or complaining.
4. If they could not find an appropriate place to eat, they would camp out and cook for themselves, or depend on the kindness of strangers they met along the way.

FEASTING ON ASPHALT

In the spring of 2006 Alton and his six-man crew began their journey at Isle of Palms, South Carolina, on the Atlantic coast. For the next six weeks, they traveled across the country, making their way through South Carolina, Georgia, North Carolina, Tennessee, Kentucky, Indiana, Missouri, Kansas, Colorado, Utah, Arizona, and Nevada, before reaching California and the Pacific Ocean.

Alton and his crew traveled by motorcycle with no specific plan in mind. His only time restriction was a work commitment later that summer. They rode day-by-day without knowing where they were going, what they would see, or where they would eat.

Alton planned on making the entire trip on his BMW R1200RT sport tour bike, his favorite mode of transporta-

A cameraman sets up a shot outside a Savannah, Georgia, diner that Alton visited in the first episode of Feasting on Asphalt.

Alton poses outside the sort of small roadside restaurant that he wanted to profile in Feasting on Asphalt.

tion. But this plan had to be revised when the group reached Nevada and he fell off his motorcycle. Brown broke his collarbone and a few ribs. He was forced to finish the trip in a rented SUV. Despite the accident, he still managed to keep his sense of humor. "The bike's OK," he told *CBS News* later. "Just a few thousand dollars worth of damage but, you know, don't drop motorcycles if you don't have to. They don't bounce."

During the journey Alton and the members of his crew sampled a variety of regional foods and dishes. These included pickled pig's feet (South Carolina), cracklin' cornbread (Georgia), kudzu (North Carolina), burgoo (Indiana), frybread (Colorado) and hard tack (California). At one point, when they were stranded in western Colorado for several hours, he even caught, cooked, and ate crickets.

By the time the trip ended, Alton's childhood memories had been reaffirmed. He reported that the people he met were as gracious and the places he visited as enjoyable as the ones he recalled from his 1969 journey. In an interview he cited the experience of being invited to share a family meal being prepared at a small hotel in Estill, South Carolina. After commenting on the pleasing aroma, Alton was invited into the motel manager's small apartment to sample the curry soup. The food was wonderful, Alton said, but he was even more impressed by the hospitality of the motel manager and his wife. "There was that one blessed ingredient: the Patels' graciousness," Alton wrote later. "Their willingness to share. Their extraordinary hospitality. In a tiny motel in Estill, I had a meal I'll never forget, and made friends I'll remember forever."

The Food Network aired *Feasting on Asphalt* as a four-part series that July and August. In the opening monologue of the first episode, Alton summarized the show's philosophy:

> Nothing plucks the heartstrings of the American spir-
> it like an open road. Oh, I'm not talking about those
> rivers of concrete, which lure us with stable speeds
> and zero surprises. I'm talking about the highways
> and byways that really stitch this crazy quilt of a coun-
> try together . . . Interstates give you culinary conform-
> ity. But out here favors change with the contours of
> land. And words like hospitality take on old meanings.

FEASTING ON ASPHALT 2: THE RIVER RUN

In the spring of 2007 Brown took the opportunity to experi-
ence some more hospitality when he and his crew returned to
the road for a second season of *Feasting on Asphalt*. This time
their 26-day journey took them along the length of the
Mississippi River. They began the thousand-mile trip in
Venice, Louisiana. The travelers then made their way through
Mississippi, Arkansas, Tennessee, Kentucky, Illinois,
Missouri, Iowa, and Wisconsin. The journey ended in
Minnesota, at Itasca State Park, which is the source of the
Mississippi River.

For *Feasting on Asphalt 2: The River Run*, Alton switched
bikes to a BMW R1200GS. Despite his previous accident, he
contended that a motorcycle was the best means of transportation for the trip. He later wrote, "Most of all, I like traveling by bike because motorcycles are wonderful icebreakers.
It's amazing to me how many times we can pull up at a place
and immediately people want to talk to us, not about food,
but about the bikes."

During the expedition, Alton and his gang sampled grilled
alligator (Louisiana), grits and headcheese (Mississippi),

Alton is surrounded by memorabilia at the Coca-Cola Museum, which he visited while filming the second Feasting on Asphalt *documentary.*

fried bologna (Tennessee), almond crème pie (Illinois), fried chicken livers (Iowa), and piroshki (Minnesota). They also visited such food-related sites as the Coca-Cola Museum, in Vicksburg, Mississippi, and the home of the creator of spinach-eating Popeye, in Chester, Illinois.

After the journey was completed, Brown returned home to his family. The trip had been a success and had taught him a valuable lesson, he wrote:

> If there is one thing I've learned, it's that the real power of food isn't in its ability to thrill or fill or surprise or please. It's in its ability to connect us to ourselves, to each other, to our heritage, to our land,

maybe to our future. Food's a road, and it can lead you to a discovery or two if you let it.

In the fall of 2007 the Food Network aired *Feasting on Asphalt 2: The River Run* as six episodes.

A fourth book by Brown evolved from the show. During the trip, Alton took dozens of photos and kept notebooks and journals. He collected his thoughts, ramblings, and photos for a new book entitled *Feasting on Asphalt: The River Run*. The book, published in 2008, included 40 original road-food recipes gathered from the restaurants he visited and the people he met. One unusual dish was "koolicles," which Alton came across in Rosedale, Mississippi. Koolicles are dill pickles that have been soaked for a week in a jar of cherry flavored Kool-Aid.

FEASTING ON WAVES

Alton followed the spirit of *Feasting on Asphalt* with a new project. This time, though, he and the crew abandoned their motorcycles and took to the seas in a pair of 50-foot catamarans. Filmed in April 2008 *Feasting on Waves* featured Brown and his crew in a journey around the Caribbean Sea. The four-part series was shot and edited on the boats.

Like the earlier shows, this *Feasting* documentary fol-

Alton has a tattoo of a skull and crossed knife and fork on his upper right arm. Below the skull is the inscription "MMVII," the Roman numeral for 2007. It stands for the year that he got the tattoo, which commemorates his *Feasting on Asphalt* motorcycle TV series.

The two boats used by Alton and his crew while filming *Feasting on Waves* were the *Chef de Mer* and *Boheme*.

lowed Alton as he searched for local specialties and delicacies—this time in the Caribbean. "I'm fascinated by the convergence of cultures there," he told Chow.com. "It really can be considered the birthplace of American cuisine."

Brown and his crew began the trip in the island of St. Kitts, in the eastern Caribbean. They journeyed through the Leeward Islands to the British Virgin Islands. Along the way, he and his crew sampled the foods native to each region and spoke to the people who produced them. Many of the foods they encountered are rarely found on the United States mainland. Among those featured on the show were taro (a root vegetable), christophine (a kind of squash), and amaranth (a leafy vegetable). The Food Network aired the four episodes of *Feasting on Waves* the following September.

Alton has not closed the door on making more Feasting programs. He told *TV Guide*, "I've been thinking that not only could there be more *Feasting on Asphalts*, there could be *Feasting on Waves*, *Feasting on Clouds*, *Feasting on Hooves*. . . . You could take this in a lot of different directions."

In 2009, Alton decided to stop eating fried and processed foods in order to lose weight and live a healthier lifestyle.

CHAPTER EIGHT

ISSUES AND CONTROVERSIES

Brown has taken a stand on some of the issues and controversies within the culinary community, as well as in the world at large. These range from the use of salt to obesity to the field of molecular gastronomy to sustainable fishing.

THE SALT CONTROVERSY

Brown has often used kosher salt in cooking, so his decision in 2009 to serve as a spokesman for Diamond Crystal kosher salt, which is owned by food giant Cargill, seemed a natural fit. However, salt—which is a combination of sodium and chloride—has gained a reputation as an unhealthy seasoning.

Since the 1970s studies have linked high sodium intake with the risk of high blood pressure, heart attack, and stroke. U.S. government dietary guidelines recommend that Americans limit sodium consumption to less than 2,300 milligrams (mg) per day (One teaspoon of table salt has 2,325 mg of sodium.) However, the average American consumes about 3,400 mg per day. Medical experts estimate that as many as 150,000 lives could be saved each year if people would cut down on the amount of salt in their diet.

Salt not only enhances the flavor of the food but also serves as a preservative. It is an important ingredient in processed foods, which include cold cuts, soups, and cheese. Processed foods typically have a high sodium content. In combination with restaurant meals, processed foods account for 80 percent of salt in the American diet.

As part of an effort to counter the negative press about salt, Cargill hired Brown to help spread the message that salt enhances food and is safe when used correctly. In a 2009 press release, the company's marketing manager stated, "Salt is a very common ingredient that leads to exceptional results in the kitchen, when used correctly. . . . We're excited for [Alton Brown] to share his expertise about Diamond Crystal salt with a broader audience of cooks so they can apply his knowledge in their own kitchens."

Cargill featured Alton in a video on a website called Salt 101. In the video he praises salt as a flavor enhancer, even on foods such as ice cream and chocolate cookies. "Salt is a pretty amazing compound," he says in the video. "So make sure you have plenty of salt in your kitchen at all times."

The video does more than promote salt as a way of enhancing the flavors in food. Through various "lessons" Brown explains the science and benefits of cooking with salt, and provides information on its history, chemical composi-

Kosher salt, obtained from evaporated seawater, has crystals that are larger, and more irregular than those of table salt, which is mined from underground salt deposits.

Alton's video for Diamond Crystal can be found at www.salt101.com.

tion, and importance in helping the body to function properly. After the website Salt 101 was launched, Alton drew criticism from many viewers who saw it as nothing more than a commercial promoting the increased use of salt.

Although Brown praises salt for bringing out flavors in food while cooking, he has also often said that the healthiest thing a person can do is cook his or her own meals. Around the same time that the salt campaign launched, a slimmed down Alton appeared in the new season of *Iron Chef America*. Part of the reason for the weight loss was his decision to never eat processed foods or fast foods.

OBESITY AND DIET

In October 2009 viewers were shocked when they saw Alton on the new season of *Iron Chef America*. His appearance had changed drastically. He had lost a lot of weight. Many fans expressed their concern about his health on Internet message boards, but Brown soon put their fears to rest. He explained that his 50-pound weight loss was not due to illness. Rather, he had undertaken a new eating regimen that had helped him lose weight over a period of eight months.

In the *Good Eats* episode entitled, "Live and Let Diet," which aired the following January, Brown gave more details. He explained that he had been inspired the previous March to lose weight after viewing tapes of himself taken at a crawfish farm in Louisiana. Disturbed at how heavy he looked, he had vowed to take off some pounds.

SARDINES AS HEALTH FOOD

Alton Brown attributes much of his weight loss to including a large amount of sardines in his diet. Sardines are small, oily herring-like fish. Whenever Alton travels, he carries a can of the tiny fish with him for every day he is on the road.

Eating the fish provides several health benefits. They have high levels of proteins and omega-3 fatty acids, which reduce the occurrence of cardiovascular disease. They are also a good source of vitamin D, calcium, vitamin B_{12}, and protein. Sardines eat mostly plants, so they do not ingest high levels of contaminants, such as mercury. Fish like salmon or tuna that consume other fish tend to accumulate high levels of contaminants in their bodies. Because sardines are short-lived, they also have less time to absorb hazardous toxins.

Rather than going on a diet, Alton explained, he had changed his eating habits. His plan called for organizing his food into four categories. The first category was made up of the foods that he could eat daily. These included fruits, whole grains, and leafy greens. The second category consisted of foods that he planned to eat three times a week. They included oily fish, yogurt, and broccoli. The third group included red meat, pasta, desserts, and alcohol—these foods could be eaten no more than once a week. And in the fourth category were foods that Alton had decided he would no longer eat at all. Fast foods, soda, processed meals, and canned soups were on this list, as well as anything labeled as "diet."

One other rule that Alton followed was that he had to eat breakfast every day, without exception. During the "Live and Let Diet" episode, he pointed out that nutritionists and doctors call breakfast the most important meal of the day. And he mentioned that several studies have found that people who lose weight and maintain weight loss are those who regularly eat breakfast.

Alton subsequently put 10 pounds back on his frame, but the added weight was in the form of muscle. Brown had begun working out with a personal trainer. His weekly exercise regimen included lifting weights, boxing, and short-distance running. In 2010 he said that he considered himself to be in the best shape of his life.

After losing so much weight, Brown began to speak out on the subject of obesity in America. He has said that he considers the high rate of obesity in the United States to be the result of negligence, rather than caused by a disease. To Alton, it is the leading health concern in the country today.

One reason for the rise in obesity, Alton has said, is the popularity of food and cooking shows on television, including his own. One show that particularly disturbed him was the Travel Channel's *Man v. Food*, which premiered in December 2008. Hosted by Adam Richman, the show features Richman visiting various cities and highlighting restaurants that are known for their "big food" preparations. Toward the end of each episode, Richman attempts a culinary challenge that requires him to eat a large quantity of food within a specified time limit. Shows have featured him trying to finish off a 72-ounce steak, 15 dozen oysters, a 7-pound breakfast burrito, and a 10-course Italian meal. Other challenges required him to eat very hot or spicy foods, such as atomic hot wings, hottest curry, and habanero chile cheese fritters.

In *Man v. Food*'s first season, the show received the highest ratings of any new program to debut on the Travel Channel. Reviews were generally favorable. Many critics

In recent years Alton has criticized television programs like Man v. Food, *which he believes encourage overeating and contribute to obesity.*

agreed with the *Star-Ledger* reporter who wrote, "It ain't deep, and it certainly ain't healthy (I could feel my arteries clog just from watching), but it's fun." Others had some reservations, and Alton was one of them. He had a strong response in September 2010, when asked by Zap2it for his opinion of *Man v. Food*: "That show is about gluttony and gluttony is wrong," he said. "It's wasteful. Think about people that are starving to death and think about that show." He continued, "I think it's an embarrassment."

Alton's comments did not sit well with Richman. He responded on Twitter, saying, "Alton Brown: MvF is about indulgence—NOT gluttony—& has brought loads of biz to Mom-n-Pop places. You were my hero, sir. No more."

Brown recognizes that celebrity chefs and the Food Network have played a role in the U.S. food culture. He told Zap2It, "I think that our culture's awareness of food is increasing. That's good. We have big problems in our food system that need to be addressed. I don't think that most of us in the media are doing as much as we could to address that. But hey, we're entertainers. By and large, that's the first thing we're here to do."

Although celebrity chefs are entertainers, he added, that does not mean they do not contribute to the problem. He explained:

> There has got to be a correlation between food media and Americans becoming big fat pigs. I'm not going to say Food Network's responsible for American obesity. I'm not going to say that because of course what you put in your mouth is your own fault and your own duty. But the fact that the rise of the celebrity chef has happened hand-in-hand with people becoming big fat pigs, someone's going to reckon with that."

MOLECULAR GASTRONOMY

Another food topic that Brown has commented on is the field of molecular gastronomy. It deals with the application of a variety of chemicals, techniques, and tools to food. An example, is the technique of spherification developed by Spanish chef Ferran Adriá. Spherification is the process of shaping a liquid, such as apple juice, into tiny caviar-like spheres. The process involves using chemical agents like sodium alginate.

Brown prefers cooking that uses basic foods and preparations. In July 2008 he told *Chemical and Engineering News*, "If you're a good chef and you want to stretch yourself to find new and interesting things to do, it can have great results. However, it can get a little freaky sometimes. The food is inedible because it's not food—it's a chemistry exam."

Some people have criticized Alton for his negative statements. They point out that his entire career has been built on the science of food. Brown responds that the difference is that he uses science to explain how and why cooking processes work. His purpose is to teach the science behind cooking to help his viewers better understand the process and become better cooks. In molecular gastronomy, chemical agents are being used to do the work itself.

Still, Alton admits that the trend has its place in the culinary world. In March 2011 he told *Baltimore Magazine*, "It breaks out of the old molds and lets us play with food." He

An internationally renowned French chemist and cook named Hervé This is known as "the father of molecular gastronomy."

has said he uses the chemicals xanthan gum in his salad dressings. But it concerns him that proponents of molecular gastronomy won't learn and understand the scientific processes of cooking. On his website he explained:

> [M]any young cooks are attempting to jump over the basics and go straight to methylcellulose, sodium alginate, various polysaccharides, gums, and even transglutaminase, which can make some very interesting sausage when properly applied. But ask them to sauté a mushroom or bake a meringue and many turn up their noses or simply lose interest. . . . I just want my food to taste, smell, and feel like food.

THE SUSTAINABLE SEAFOOD INITIATIVE

Yet another food-related issue that concerns Brown is the great population loss of certain species of fish. Americans consume a large number of a relatively few species of fish, such as blue fin tuna, salmon, and grouper. They, along with Atlantic cod, red snapper, Chilean sea bass, and swordfish, are considered threatened species. In fact, throughout the world the populations of one-third of all fished species have collapsed.

Brown is working to raise awareness of this problem and to educate people to purchase only sustainable seafood—that is, to buy and cook fish whose populations are not threatened. In August 2011, he was in Chattanooga, where along with the Tennessee Aquarium's Conservation Institute he helped launch the sustainable seafood initiative. The long-term initiative aims to educate and encourage people to buy and eat sustainable seafood.

The August event highlighted five sustainable species: American Lobster, oyster, yellow tail snapper, catfish, and

Alton is interested in teaching people about sustainable fishing practices, in order to preserve rapidly declining stocks of wild fish.

rainbow trout. In an effort to encourage the consumption of these species, Brown developed recipes that featured them. The following month, he planned to return to host an event in which restaurant chefs from the area would offer additional dishes featuring sustainable seafood. Brown explained, "I will be working with all of the chefs and wait staffs, because a lot of the selling of sustainable seafood is in the education and narrative. Then we're going to turn it over to these chefs to put their creativity on display and show the real culinary possibilities of these fish."

CHAPTER NINE

ALTON BROWN THE MAN

Through the popularity of *Good Eats* and other Food Network shows, Alton Brown has become a media celebrity. But unlike most other personalities on the Food Network, he does not consider himself a chef. Rather, he calls himself a filmmaker who makes shows about food.

Regardless of his title, Brown has earned a good living through his television programs, books, personal appearances, and endorsements. Although he enjoys the monetary benefits of being a Food Network TV personality, Alton knows what really matters in his life. In October 2010 he told *USA Today*, "The stuff that's important, your work, your family—that's tangible. Everything else is frosting . . . cake is great with frosting, but if the frosting's gone, you've got to make sure the cake is good, too."

HOME LIFE

Through the years Alton has occasionally shared his family with *Good Eats* viewers. His mother and grandmother

Alton is careful to allow plenty of time for his family, which he says makes him more effective in his work.

appeared in a few episodes of the regular series. And daughter Zoey appeared on the show more than a dozen times. Often referred to as "Alton's Spawn," Zoey made her debut in season three in the episode on cabbage, "Head Games." Two other "family" members seen on *Good Eats*—Alton's sister Marsha and his evil twin brother B.A.—were both nothing more than products of his vivid imagination.

However, Alton's wife, DeAnna was seldom seen on *Good Eats*. She appeared only briefly in the episode "Behind the Eats" and in the special anniversary show "Good Eats Turns 10." But she was an important part of the program, serving behind the scenes since season five as the program's executive producer, and handling the business operations of the show's production company, Be Square Productions. In addition to producing *Good Eats*, the company worked on *Cooking Thin* and *Feasting on Waves*. It also produced film projects for General Electric and Whole Foods, among others.

The Brown family has lived since 2006 in a 7,500-foot historic mansion in Marietta, Georgia. Before Alton became a success, the couple used to drive by the house and imagine what it would be like to live there. When she felt they had enough money to buy the place, DeAnna handled the real estate negotiations. Alton explained, "My deal with DeAnna was, 'I'll sign the papers, but don't ever tell me what the purchase price was.' I can't ever know, because I can't deal with that level of stress. If she says we can afford it, we can afford it."

A year after moving in, Alton was still raving about the home, telling a reporter with *Atlanta Magazine*, "It's huge. There are wings. It's got grounds. It's spectacular. I'm in love with this house."

Alton often credits DeAnna for his success. In a 2008 interview he said, "To this day, she's a full-time mom and she runs this company full-time. Lawyers, insurance, accountants, all the money. All of that. She basically has made it her professional mission to give me what I need to do this work. There's absolutely no question it could not be done without her. She's the business."

In the same interview, Alton said that he and his wife shared cooking responsibilities at home "almost 50-50." But with a young daughter and his many responsibilities, he admitted that he was not always able to get home in time to make dinner. So DeAnna often picked up the slack.

FAMILY PRIVACY

Alton does not share much information about his wife and daughter; he feels strongly about protecting their privacy. When they accompany him to public events, he insists that

Alton lives in Marietta, Georgia, with his wife DeAnna and their daughter Zoey. He prefers to keep his family out of the public's eye.

people leave them alone and not take their picture. He explained on his website: "I'm quasi-famous, they're not. They enjoy certain rights I have sacrificed by choosing to be a cable-ebrity and as a husband and father I will protect their rights to the fullest."

Brown was infuriated in mid-2011 when his family's privacy was invaded online. He had opened a Twitter account in May, but he closed it down after only a couple of months. In early August he explained on his blog why he stopped. "I left Twitter because a parasitic troll fraudulently posing as my wife started tweeting," he wrote. "It even used a photo of my family as its avatar."

Alton explained later that he was very disturbed that the person posing as DeAnna used a family photo. "I always want to protect my daughter Zoey," he said. "I blew a gasket. If they had done anything but use that picture, I would have laughed it off. . . . That crossed the line."

About a month after leaving Twitter, Alton changed his mind. Upon his return to Twitter, he announced on his blog, "It turns out the sick, lowlife . . . population on Twitter is actually rather low while the number of nice, normal . . . folks is relatively high . . . You win. My people have talked to Twitter's people and as of today I'm back."

A MAN OF FAITH

Brown is a member of the Johnson Ferry Baptist Church in Marietta, Georgia. In 2007 he told *Atlanta Magazine*, "The single biggest life-changing thing for me is I just got baptized. . . . Everything else pales in comparison to acceptance of Christianity. That's number one."

Alton's faith plays an important role in his work as well as in his personal life. "One of the things I pray for on a daily basis," he said in September 2010, "is that whatever God wants me to be doing, it's reflected through my actions, how I deal with other people, the way I do my job. And I hope I do it in a way that pleases Him."

One of the actions that Brown takes is helping others through Heifer International. He has donated book royalties and money to the organization, which helps lift people out of poverty. In 2010 he made a public service announcement for the group, in which he explained how Heifer International works—that making a donation of an animal to a family is like giving it a small business. The wool, milk, or eggs the animal produces becomes income, producing a sustainable livelihood for that family.

THE END OF GOOD EATS

In May 2011 Alton Brown was honored with a James Beard Foundation award for Best TV Food Personality for his show *Good Eats*. Fellow nominees for the award were chef Bobby Flay, the host of *Brunch @ Bobby's*, and pastry chef Duff Goldman, of *Ace of Cakes*. That same month Alton announced that after 14 seasons and 249 episodes, as well as several specials, *Good Eats* would be coming to an end.

A few months later Brown said in an interview, "I feel after 250 I can walk away from that library of work and feel good about it and know it's had an effect to some degree on somebody besides me and those who worked on it. And it will hold its own for a while. We wanted to make sure they were dense, juicy and succulent and last a long time." He noted that the six-year-old set was being dismantled, although he would keep a few props such as the paper maché chicken for himself.

The hit show wrapped up filming that September. The second-to-last *Good Eats* project was another Thanksgiving

GOOD EATS TOPICS

When Alton announced the end of *Good Eats* in May 2011, *Chicago Tribune* reporter Steve Cavendish published a complete list of all the topics that had been covered in the series. Examples include:

A apples, angel food cake, artichokes, avocado, asparagus

B biscuits, butter, bacon, buttercream frosting, beets

C chocolate, canning, coffee, corn, cabbage

D duck, dip, doughnuts, dill pickles, dried fruit

E eggs, eggplant, energy bar, eggnog, espresso

F fruitcake, fondue, fish and chips, French omelet, fudge

G grilled cheese, garlic, gelatin, grains, grits

H ham, honey, home brewing, herbs, hollandaise sauce

I ice cream

J Japanese ingredients

K knives

L lobster, lemon meringue pie, leeks, lentils, lasagna

M mushrooms, mussels, mayonnaise, macaroni and cheese, muffins

N nuts

O onion soup, oats, oysters, olives, okra

P potatoes, pasta, pilaf, pie crust, pomegranate

Q quiche

R ravioli, roulade, rice, roasted chicken, roux

S steak, salad, shrimp, squid, strawberries

T tofu, tea, tuna, tomato, tortillas

V vinegar, vanilla

W wonton, waffle, water, whole fish, wood-fired pizzas

Y yogurt, yellow cake, yeast rolls

special to be aired in November. The final *Good Eats* episode was an hour-long special on dark chocolate. Repeats of the program were to run on the Cooking Channel, a spinoff of the Food Network. Meanwhile, Alton's face continued to be seen on the Food Network as season four of *The Next Iron Chef* premiered that October.

New Projects

Having ended the *Good Eats* run, Alton has turned his attention to other projects. In the past he has expressed interest in projects that would make people more aware of food issues. He envisioned a series of documentaries on subjects such as food irradiation, genetic engineering, and food-borne illnesses. In a March 2008 interview with the *Buffalo News*, he said that for several years he had been interested in working on projects about serious food issues such as sustainability. "But the thing that we have to do is that we also have to make it entertaining," he noted. "That's the challenge . . . It's one of the things I'm most looking forward to, the next decade of my career."

Alton has also said he would like to work on a project for schools on food and food choices. He once told the *St. Petersburg Times*, "I have the dream of finding funding to do an educational series—not for television, but for classroom application—about food. I'm really alarmed about the way that kids, especially teenagers, think about food. . . . They absorb adults' bad attitudes about food. I'd very much more like to get into education."

Alton is committed to continuing to work with the Food Network. In March 2011 he agreed to a new contract that extended his partnership with the network for three more years. At the time he said, "Food is a great subject for a filmmaker and Food Network has been a great home. They provide me with a level of creative support and professional commitment that would be tough to find anywhere else in the industry. I'm juiced to have an opportunity to continue the good work we've established over the last dozen years and to look ahead to new projects."

In October 2011, in an interview with *Eater National*, Brown described some of the projects he had under development. He said he had two shows in development with the Food Network. One was a miniseries called *Foods That Changed the World*. It would give the background story of particular foods that influenced history. He also described another show called *Food Files*. "It will be just kind of a fun investigation of a particular food topic," Alton explained.

Alton plans to continue working with the Food Network on shows such as Food Network Star, *on which he has appeared as a guest judge several times. Here, he offers advice to Jeff Mauro at the Farmers Market during the show's seventh season, which aired in 2011. He is also developing new programs for the Food Network.*

Brown was honored in 2009 by Monterey Bay Aquarium's Cooking for Solutions as "Educator of the Year."

"You know, why can't we stay on a diet? How are we going to feed 9 billion people? What does "sustainable" really mean?"

Brown also discussed a plan to launch a series of e-book cookbooks and his goal to produce a documentary or a book on the history of cookbooks. Another interest would be a documentary on the history of cooking shows. But that would be a more difficult project to accomplish, he said, since many tapes of shows going back to the early days of TV no longer exist. And many of the ones that do exist have legal issues that would block him from using them. "I don't know how that project's going to come together," Brown noted. "I might have to be retired from my TV career before I dive into that one."

Alton also told the *Tampa Tribune* that a possible future project would be a cooking show for kids. He noted, "I never designed [*Good Eats*] to be kid-friendly, but it certainly seems to be what happened. If anyone is going to turn America into more of a cooking nation and less of a consuming nation, it's going to be kids." And Alton Brown would be happy to teach them.

p. 7: "The Award is determined . . ." "The Mission of the Peabody Awards," Peabody Awards, http://www.peabody.uga.edu/mission.php

p. 8: "Good Eats isn't about . . ." "Alton Brown: 10 Years of 'Good Eats,'" NPR (October 11, 2009). http://www.npr.org/templates/story /story.php?storyId=113624708

p. 11: "What sets Brown and . . ." *Good Eats* 2006," Peabody Awards, http://www.peabody.uga.edu/winners/details.php?id=1454

p. 12: "I'm blown away to . . ." Allyson Mann, "The Nutty Professor," *Georgia Magazine* (June 2008). http://www.uga.edu/gm/artman/publish/0709brown.html

p. 12: "Without question, this is the . . ." Ibid.

p. 13: "My mom was a charming . . ." Virginia Parker, "Alton Brown Steaks His Claim," *Atlanta Magazine* (April 2007). http://www.goodeatsfanpage.com/abfp/ABArticles/2007-04_ATL_mag.htm

p. 14: "We drove and drove . . ." Alton Brown, "Food for Thought," *Guideposts* (August 2006). http://www.goodeatsfanpage.com /abfp/ABArticles/2006-07-26.htm

p. 15: "I saw scenery that . . ." Ibid.

p. 15: "Though Al Brown's untimely death . . ." *White County News* (May 25, 2006). http://www.goodeatsfanpage.com/abfp/ABArticles /WhiteCountyNews2006.htm

p. 15: "Being a male in . . ." Parker, "Alton Brown Steaks His Claim."

p. 16: "Ma Mae wasn't a great . . ." Alton Brown, "Rants and Raves" (December 4, 2001). http://www.goodeatsfanpage.com /ABFP/ABTimeline/MaMae.htm

p. 16: "As a youth I was . . ." Alton Brown, "Rants and Raves," (June 10, 2003). http://www.altonbrown.com/pages/rants.html

p. 17: "Truth is, I was a . . ." Chris Rywalt, "Add Apples for Flavor," *Macworld Magazine* (March 1, 2001). http://www.macworld.com/article/1994/2001/03/buzzbrown.html

p. 17: "I'd like to think . . ." Jackie Micucci, "Upfront: Good Specs," *20/20* (September 2003). http://www.2020mag.com/story/297/

p. 18: "It was an extremely lean . . ." Mann, "The Nutty Professor."

p. 19: "Yeah, cooking in college . . ." Michael Menninger, "My Interview with Alton Brown," Good Eats Fan Page, 2002. http://www.goodeatsfanpage.com/References/TheInterviews/MyABInterview/ABInterview4.htm

p. 19: "It was the cultural significance . . ." Corinne A. Marasco, "An Appetite For Science," *Chemical and Engineering News* (July 28, 2008). http://pubs.acs.org/cen/science/86/8630sci8.html

p. 20: "I understand now that . . ." Parker, "Alton Brown Steaks His Claim."

p. 21: "I really did not like . . ." Lori Lundquist, "Some Like It Hot," *Channel Guide Magazine* (June 5, 2003).

p. 22:   "When his television show . . ." Alton Brown, "Best Cookbooks," *Wall Street Journal*, February 6, 2010, http://online.wsj.com/article /SB10001424052748704107204575039311414125360.html#articleTa bs%3Darticle

p. 22:   "Nobody was giving us any . . ." India Powell, "Food for Thought," *Atlanta Home Improvement* (October 2004).

p. 23:   "We went from making a . . ." Lundquist, "Some Like It Hot."

p. 24:   "When I started learning how . . ." Pamela Davis, "The Mad Scientist of the Kitchen," *St. Petersburg Times* (March 21, 2002).

p. 25:   "The one book that changed . . ." Marasco, "An Appetite for Science."

p. 26:   "The internships that I did . . ." Lundquist, "Some Like It Hot."

p. 26:   "[Matecat] understood that to be . . ." Menninger, "My Interview with Alton Brown."

p. 27:   "I did my time in . . ." Genevieve Koski, "Alton Brown," *A.V. Club* (October 9, 2009). http://www.avclub.com/articles/alton-brown,33872/

p. 27:   "All at once I could . . ." Brown, "Food for Thought."

p. 30:   "I chose steak for our . . ." Alton Brown, *Good Eats: The Early Years* (New York: Stewart, Tabori and Chang, 2009), pp. 12, 16.

p. 31:   "We kind of agreed to . . ." Rywalt, "Add Apples for Flavor."

p. 31:   "[T]his PBS series . . ." Steve Johnson, "Good Eats," *Chicago Tribune* (July 17, 1998). http://articles.chicagotribune.com/1998-07-17/fea-tures/9807170374_1_meat-camera-alton-brown

p. 32:   "They liked the process I . . ." Brown, "Food for Thought."

p. 33:   "I'll come up with a . . ." Michael Menninger, "My Interview with Alton Brown: Creation Process Questions," Good Eats Fan Page, http://www.goodeatsfanpage.com/References/TheInterviews/MyABInte rview/ABInterview1.htm

p. 34:   "My show is heavily researched . . ." Don Fernandez, "My Bookmarks," *Atlanta Journal-Constitution* (June 19, 2001).

p. 34:   "I kind of quickly moved . . ." Rywalt, "Add Apples for Flavor."

p. 34:   "You've got certain tools that . . ." Ibid.

p. 34:   "It took me a long . . ." Lundquist, "Some Like It Hot."

p. 37:   "Our first requirement was that . . ." Willis Barton, "Primetime Kitchen," *Home Magazine* (Summer 2003). http://www.goodeatsfan-page.com/abfp/ABArticles/PrimetimeKitchen.htm

p. 38:   "We've made changes to the . . ." Menninger, "My Interview with Alton Brown: General Questions."

p. 40:   "Comedy is real hard. When . . ." Ibid.

p. 40:   "Highbrow, lowbrow, I don't think . . ." Ibid.

p. 40:   ""I have the best people . . ." Menninger, "My Interview with Alton Brown: Creation Process Questions."

p. 42:   "Alton Brown . . . transformed . . ." "The 2004 Bon Appétit Awards: Cooking Teacher: Alton Brown," *Bon Appétit*, 2004. http://prod.bonap-petit.com/magazine/baawards/2008/10/baa_2004?currentPage=6

p. 43:   "I literally locked . . ." Steve Litscher, "Chef Alton Brown of 'Good Eats': Writer, Director, Food Hacker and Gear Head," *Roadfly* (October 6, 2004). http://www.roadfly.com/magazine/14/alton_brown.3.html

p. 44:   "Alton Brown brings an MTV . . ." *Publishers Weekly* review.

http://www.amazon.com/Im-Just-Here-Food-Cooking/dp/B001H55MWS /ref=sr_1_2?s=books&ie=UTF8&qid=1315247475&sr=1-2

p. 44:   "I don't have a restaurant . . ." Chris Krewson, "Food-Science Geek," *Morning Call* (May 28, 2003). http://www.goodeatsfanpage.com/abfp/ABArticles/mcall.htm

p. 45:   "I love cooking because the . . ." Wes Marshall, "Alton Brown Is Coming to Town," *Austin Chronicle* (March 28, 2003). http://www.goodeatsfanpage.com/abfp/ABArticles/AustinChronicle.htm

p. 46:   "Like MacGyver, I get great . . ." Alton Brown, *Alton Brown's Gear For Your Kitchen* (New York: Stewart, Tabori and Chang, 2003), p. 7.

p. 47:   "Brown has all the . . ." *Publishers Weekly* review. http://www.amazon.com /Alton-Browns-Gear-Your-Kitchen/dp/1584796960/ref=sr_1_1?s= books&ie=UTF8&qid=1315248032&sr=1-1

p. 48:   "I realized that with baking . . ." Litscher, "Chef Alton Brown of 'Good Eats': Writer, Director, Food Hacker and Gear Head."

p. 49:   "I spent three months . . ." Parker, "Alton Brown Steaks His Claim."

p. 51:   "The grape in question is . . ." Alton Brown Joins Welch's in Standing Up to Free Radicals," PRNewswire (November 11, 2008). http://multivu.prnewswire.com/mnr/welchs/35871/

p. 58:   "One of the reasons that . . ." Lori Acken, "Alton Brown Dishes Season 2 of 'The Next Iron Chef' . . . And Why a Jellyfish Is Not Good Eats," *Channel Guide Magazine* (October 2009). http://channelguidemag.zap2it.com/articles/alton_brown_next_iron_chef_1009.php

p. 58:   "*Iron Chef America* is simple . . ." Ibid.

p. 59:   "You could compete on *Iron* . . ." Ibid.

p. 59:   "The Next Iron Chef operates . . ." Joshua David Stein, "Alton Brown on Being a Vessel, *Next Iron Chef*, and His Faith," *Eater National* (September 28, 2010). http://eater.com/archives/2010/09/28/altonbrown-on-next-iron-chef-faith-vessel.php

p. 61:   "I'm very excited to lend . . ." "Announcements: Brown and Cora," *Iron Chef America: Supreme Cuisine*, http://www.ironchefamericagame.com/

p. 61:   "Alton Brown is the lone . . ." Chris Watters, "*Iron Chef America: Supreme Cuisine* Review," *GameSpot* (January 8, 2009). http://www.gamespot.com/wii/action/ironchef/review.html

p. 63:   "We've enhanced some dishes, added . . ." *Brown, Good Eats: The Early Years*, p. 9.

p. 63:   "They're actually some of my . . ." Hanh Nguyen, "Alton Brown Talks 'Good Eats 2' Celebrity Chefs," Zap2it, http://blog.zap2it.com/frominsidethebox/2010/09/alton-brown-talks-good-eats-2-celebrity-chefs.html

p. 66:   "When I fly, I may . . ." Wilson Rothman, "Food Network's Alton Brown Talks to Giz: Caribbean Adventuring with a Garmin, an iPhone and a Shload of Cameras," *Gizmodo* (September 6, 2008). http://gizmodo.com/5046242/food-networks-alton-brown-talks-to-giz-caribbeanadventuring-with-a-garmin-an-iphone-and-a-shload-of-cameras?comment=7630179

p. 66:   "deathly afraid of me . . ." Litscher, "Chef Alton Brown of 'Good Eats': Writer, Director, Food Hacker and Gear Head."

p. 66:   "One of the great things . . ." Ibid.

p. 68:   "To this day I believe . . ." Alton Brown, *Feasting on Asphalt: The River Run* (New York: Stewart, Tabori and Chang, 2008), p. 8.

p. 68:   "To tell you the truth . . ." Brown, "Food for Thought."

p. 71:   "The bike's OK. Just a . . ." Amy Bonawitz, "Alton Brown Hits the American Road," CBS News (February 11, 2009). http://www.cbsnews.com/stories/2006/08/01/entertainment/main1853445.shtml

p. 71:   "There was that one blessed . . ." Brown, "Food for Thought."

p. 72:   "Nothing plucks the heartstrings of . . ." "Feasting on Asphalt: Opening Monologue," *Feasting on Asphalt*, http://feastingonasphalt.altonbrownfans.com/

p. 72:   "Most of all, I . . ." Brown, *Feasting on Asphalt: The River Run*, p. 10.

p. 73:   "If there is one thing . . ." Ibid., p. 196.

p. 75:   "I'm fascinated by the convergence . . ." Louisa Chu, "Crushing Bones with Alton Brown," Chow.com (April 11, 2008). http://www.chow.com/food-news/54454/crushing-bones-with-alton-brown/

p. 75:   "I've been thinking that not . . ." Matt Webb Mitovich, "Food TV's Good Eats Guy Hits the Road," *TVGuide.com* (July 2006). http://www.goodeatsfanpage.com/abfp/ABArticles/images/fromTVGuide2006-07.htm

p. 78:   "Salt is a very common . . ." Alton Brown Shares Culinary Wit and Wisdom Through 'Salt 101' Campaign," PRNewswire (November 18, 2009). http://www.prnewswire.com/news-releases/alton-brown-shares-culinary-wit-and-wisdom-through-salt-101-campaign-70371602.html

p. 78:   "Salt is a pretty amazing . . ." Michael Moss, "The Hard Sell on Salt" *New York Times* (May 29, 2010), p. A1.

p. 83:   "It ain't deep, and it . . ." Alan Sepinwall, "Me Want Food!," NJ.com (December 31, 2008). http://www.nj.com/entertainment/tv/index.ssf/2008/12/me_want_food.html

p. 83:   "That show is about . . ." Rosemary Black, "Alton Brown Disses Adam Richman's 'Man vs. Food'; Calls It 'Disgusting,' and 'Embarrassment,'" *New York Daily News* (September 29, 2010). http://articles.nydailynews.com/2010-09-29/entertainment/27076731_1_travel-channel-gluttony-adam-richman

p. 83:   "Alton Brown: MvF is about . . ." Ibid.

p. 83:   "I think that our culture's . . ." Nguyen, "Alton Brown Talks 'Good Eats 2' Celebrity Chefs."

p. 83:   "There has got to be . . ." Ibid.

p. 84:   "If you're a good chef . . ." Marasco, "An Appetite for Science."

p. 84:   "It breaks out of the . . ." Suzanne Loudermilk, "Alton Brown Talks About Owning Planes, His Corn-on-the-Cob Eating Style, and Coming to Baltimore," *Baltimore Magazine* (March 3, 2011). http://www.baltimoremagazine.net/ingoodtaste/2011/03/alton-brown-talks-about-owning-planes-his-corn-on-the-cob-eating-style-and-comin

p. 85:   "[M]any young cooks . . ." Alton Brown, "Upon the Matter of Molecular Gastronomy" (August 18, 2011) http://altonbrown.com/2011/08/upon-the-matter-of-molecular-gastronomy/

p. 87: "I will be working with . . ." Mary Barnett, "Chef Alton Brown Helps Launch Sustainable Seafood Initiative in Chattanooga," Nooga.com, Scripps Networks Interactive (August 17, 2011). http://www.scripp-snetworks.com/newsitem.aspx?id=590

p. 88: "The stuff that's important, your . . ." Brian Truitt, "Alton Brown Barely Has Time to Enjoy His 'Good Eats' Green," *USA Today* (October 10, 2010). http://www.usatoday.com/life/people/2010-10-10-alton-brown_N.htm

p. 90: "My deal with DeAnna was . . ." Parker, "Alton Brown Steaks His Claim."

p. 90: "It's huge. There are wings . . ." Ibid.

p. 90: "To this day, she's a . . ." Andrew Galarneau, "A Few More Bites from Alton Brown," BuffaloNews.com (March 5, 2008). http://www.buf-falonews.com/life/taste/article106668.ece

p. 92: "I'm quasi-famous, they're not . . ." Alton Brown, "My Fanifesto" (September 19, 2011). http://altonbrown.com/2011/09/my-fanifesto/

p. 92: "I left Twitter because a . . ." Chris Richardson, "Alton Brown's Twitter Meltdown," Web Pro News (August 8, 2011). http://www.webpronews.com/alton-browns-twitter-meltdown-2011-08

p. 92: "I always want to . . ." Rodney Ho, "Exclusive Interview with Alton Brown as He Wraps Up 'Good Eats,'" *Radio and TV Talk* (August 26, 2011). http://blogs.ajc.com/radio-tv-talk/2011/08/26/exclusive-inter-view-with-alton-brown-as-he-wraps-up-good-eats/

p. 92: "It turns out the sick . . ." Alton Brown, "Waffle, Anyone?" (August 31, 2011). http://altonbrown.com/2011/08/waffle-anyone/

p. 92: "The single biggest life-changing . . ." Parker, "Alton Brown Steaks His Claim."

p. 92: "One of the things I . . ." Stein, "Alton Brown on Being a Vessel, *Next Iron Chef*, and His Faith."

p. 93: "I feel after 250 . . ." Ho, "Exclusive Interview with Alton Brown as He Wraps Up 'Good Eats.'"

p. 95: "But the thing . . ." Galarneau, "A Few More Bites from Alton Brown."

p. 95: "I have the dream of . . ." Davis, "The Mad Scientist of the Kitchen."

p. 95: "Food is a great subject . . ." Food Network and Alton Brown Embark on New Three-Year Deal," Scripps Networks Interactive (March 28, 2011). http://newsroom.scrippsnetworks.com/article_display.cfm?arti-cle_id=4813

p. 96: "It will be just kind . . ." Raphael Brion, "Alton Brown on the *Next Iron Chef* and Future Plans," *Eater National* (October 26, 2011). http://eater.com/archives/2011/10/26/alton-brown-on-the-next-iron-chef-and-future-plans.php

p. 97: ""I don't know how . . ." Ibid.

p. 97: "I never designed . . ." Jeff Houck, "Food Network's Alton Brown in Brandon Tonight," *Tampa Tribune* (October 27, 2011). http://www2.tbo.com/news/breaking-news/2011/oct/27/3/food-net-works-alton-brown-in-brandon-tonight-ar-298613/

CHRONOLOGY

1962: Alton Crawford Brown Jr. is born in Los Angeles, California, on July 30.

1969: Brown's family moves to Cleveland, Georgia.

1997: Brown graduates from the New England Culinary Institute in Montpelier, Vermont.

1998: The pilot episode of *Good Eats* airs on the PBS station, WTTW, in Chicago.

1999: On July 7 *Good Eats* makes its debut on the Food Network.

2000: Daughter Zoey is born in January.

2002: Brown's first book, *I'm Just Here for the Food*, is published.

2003: *I'm Just Here for the Food* wins the James Beard Award for best cookbook in the reference category.

2004: Brown is named Bon Appetit's Cooking Teacher of the Year.

2005: Brown takes on a second show for the Food Network as host of *Iron Chef America*.

2006: *Feasting on Asphalt* debuts on the Food Network on July 29.

2007: *Good Eats* is honored with a 2006 Peabody Award on June 4 in New York City; in October *The Next Iron Chef* debuts, with Brown as host.

2008: Brown publishes the book *Feasting on Asphalt: The River Run*.

2009: *Good Eats* celebrates its 10-year anniversary; Brown publishes the first of his cookbook trilogy, *Good Eats: The Early Years*.

2010: The second of Brown's trilogy, *Good Eats 2: The Middle Years,* is released.

2011: In May Brown announces that *Good Eats* is ending its run, and Brown wins the James Beard Award for TV Food Personality/Host for Good Eats. In September *Good Eats 3: The Later Years* is published.

BOLSTER—the place on a knife where the blade meets the handle.

CATAMARAN—a boat with two parallel hulls.

CINEMATOGRAPHY—the art of movie photography, including both the shooting and the development of film.

CUISINE—a style of cooking that is characteristic of a particular country or region.

CULINARY—having to do with cooking and the kitchen.

ENTRÉE—the main dish or course.

FREE RADICALS—unstable molecules that attempt to bond with others to increase their stability.

HARD TACK—hard dry bread or biscuit made from flour, water and sometimes salt.

IRRADIATION—the process of exposing food to radiation to destroy microorganisms, bacteria, or viruses.

KUDZU—a fast-growing climbing plant of the pea family.

MOLECULAR GASTRONOMY—the field that deals with the application of chemicals, techniques and tools to cooking.

ROYALTY—a sum of money paid to an author for each copy of a book sold.

STEADICAM—a camera attached to the cameraman by a mechanical harness that reduces the effects of the operator's movement.

GLOSSARY

TRIVECTION OVEN—an oven that cooks by combining radiant heat, convection and microwaves.

UNITASKER—an object with only one function.

VELCRO—a fastener consisting of two strips of thin plastic sheet, one covered with tiny loops and the other with tiny flexible hooks, which adhere when pressed together.

Brown, Alton. *Alton Brown's Gear for Your Kitchen*. New York: Stewart, Tabori and Chang, 2008.

———. *Feasting on Asphalt: The River Run*. New York: Stewart, Tabori and Chang, 2008.

———. *Good Eats 3: The Later Years*. New York: Stewart, Tabori and Chang, 2011.

———. *I'm Just Here for the Food: Food + Heat = Cooking*. New York: Stewart, Tabori and Chang, 2002.

Corriher, Shirley O. *CookWise: The Secrets of Cooking Revealed*. New York: HarperCollins, 2011.

McGee, Harold. *On Food and Cooking: The Science and Lore of the Kitchen*. New York: Scribner, 2004.

INTERNET RESOURCES

HTTP:// ALTONBROWN.COM

The official website of Food Network personality Alton Brown includes a biography and his personal blog.

HTTP://WWW.FOODNETWORK.COM

The official website of the Food Network contains information about network shows, chefs, and recipes.

HTTP://WWW.MOLECULARGASTRONOMYNETWORK.COM

The website of the Molecular Gastronomy Network links to a list of popular additives used in molecular gastronomy, as well as recipes, information on training, and a community forum.

HTTP:// WWW.NECI.EDU

The official website of the New England Culinary Institute includes information about the faculty and staff, courses of study, and admission procedures.

HTTP://WWW.PEABODY.UGA.EDU

The official website of the George Foster Peabody Awards includes a history of the award and lists of all winners.

Publisher's Note: The websites listed on these pages were active at the time of publication. The publisher is not responsible for websites that have changed their address or discontinued operation since the date of publication.

Numbers in **bold italics** refer to captions.

JOHN F. GRABOWSKI is a native of Brooklyn, New York. He holds a bachelor's degree in psychology from City College of New York and a master's degree in educational psychology from Teachers College, Columbia University. He was a teacher for 39 years, as well as a freelance writer, specializing in the fields of sports, education, and comedy.

Grabowski's published work includes 55 books; a nationally syndicated sports column; consultation on several math textbooks; articles for newspapers, magazines, and the programs of professional sports teams; and comedy material sold to Jay Leno, Joan Rivers, Yakov Smirnoff, and numerous other comics. He and his wife, Patricia, live in Staten Island with their daughter, Elizabeth.